The Situation of Poetry

The Situation of Poetry

Four Essays on the Relations between Poetry, Mysticism, Magic, and Knowledge

Jacques and Raïssa Maritain

PHILOSOPHICAL LIBRARY NEW YORK

Translated from the original French *Situation de la Poésie*
by Marshall Suther.

Printed in the United States of America
By The Haddon Craftsmen, Inc.

The title of this little book may be understood in two senses: it refers to the situation of poetry within the structure of the spirit, within that complex organization of mysterious energies and virtues in the human being; and it refers also to the situation in time, insofar as the poetry of today may indicate, at this fleeting moment, virtualities which perhaps have a chance of passing into existence tomorrow. It is according to these two senses employed together that poetry is here considered.

Contents

Translator's Note

WRITING OUT OF A WIDER ACQUAINTANCE WITH FRENCH literature than with any other, and intending their work originally for a French audience, it would in any case be natural that the authors should draw most of their illustrative references from French sources. This might be the occasion of some difficulty for English-speaking readers, although not an insurmountable one when it is a matter of poets like Baudelaire, Rimbaud, Verlaine, Nerval, and others, who are surely no longer exclusively "French" poets. In the case of poets less well-known to English-speaking readers, this book would have served one of its possible functions if it helped to awaken interest in them to the point of first-hand exploration.

But it may be suggested that there is another, and not at all accidental, reason for this predominance of reference to French poetry in the present work—that the "situation" of poetry, as it has developed in the last 150 years or so, especially in its becoming conscious of itself *as poetry,* is to be seen with peculiar clarity in the work of the French poets. The role played by the French Symbolists, for instance, as "poets' poets" for a later generation of writers in English as well as French would lend weight to this view. Though early instances of a consciousness in some sort new of the special role of the poet as "ravisher of fire" are not lacking in English—one thinks of Blake, of Coleridge, of Shelley—

it would not be too surprising if it were possible to trace the development with somewhat greater precision among the French. In any case, the application of the concepts herein set forth to poetry in English should be a rewarding endeavor.

M. S.

RAÏSSA MARITAIN

Sense and Non-Sense in Poetry

WHAT I SHALL ATTEMPT TO TREAT OF HERE IS *logical sense* and *non-sense in poetry,* and also of *poetic sense.*

Logical sense, or rational sense, is not to be required in poetry for its own sake; it seems even to be extrinsic to poetry as such. And yet, in one way or another, to some degree, it always accompanies the poetic work: either in an explicit way, or in appealing implicitly to the cooperation of the intelligence. Otherwise, poetry itself disappears. That is the paradox which we should like to consider.

The *poetic sense* is one with the poetry itself. If I employ this expression here, rather than the word "poetry," it is to indicate that the poetry, or "poetic sense," causes the poem to be, by being the *form* (in Aristotelian language) or the *idea* (in the language of Spinoza) of this body, by giving it a substantial signification, an ontological sense. This *poetic sense* is quite another thing than the intelligible sense, just as the soul of a man is quite another thing than his discourse; and in the poetic work, the poetic sense is inseparable from the formal structure of the work: whether the work be clear or obscure, the poetic sense is there, whatever may become of the intelligible sense; the poetic sense is substantially bound to the form, immanent in the organization of the words, immanent in the poetic form. It cannot be separated from the verbal form which it animates from within. To "tell the story" of a poem, even the clearest of poems, is to abolish the poetry. And the sense one draws from it, in paraphrasing it, is no longer the sense of the poem. The sense of the poem is one with its verbal form.[1] (That certain verbal "correspondences" are possible from one language to another does not contradict this assertion.) This is what first of all distinguishes the poem from all works in the prosaic mode—I do not say from all prose. In the prosaic mode, indeed, the words are almost exclusively only *signs;* they are there above all to refer the mind to what they signify; they have in themselves only a secondary importance. In poetry, on the other hand, the words are at the same time signs and *objects* (objects that are carriers of images) which are organized in a living and independent body; they cannot give place to synonyms without causing the sense of the poem to suffer or die. That is why the majority of great poets cannot be translated: thus it is with Dante, Racine, Pushkin, Baudelaire, and with many others. The untranslatableness of their work is

[1] Cf. Boris de Schloezer, "La Musique, Art Méconnu," *Mesures,* 15 January, 1937. "This abstraction is only possible in the spoken language because of the fact that the content-form relation is, in this case, a transcendental relation, while in music the content or sense is found to be immanent to the form. But between these two extremes there is poetic language, which can be called 'musical' not insofar as it sounds harmonious and pleases the ear, as is ordinarily supposed, but insofar as what it signifies, its content, is immanent to its form. The pleasure, the sonorous caress, is only an accessory phenomenon, not at all necessary, for a text can be 'musical' in the sense I mean (the only acceptable sense to my way of thinking) and yet be hard on the ear. In this sense, music appears to us as the limit (in the mathematical sense of the term) of poetry; the limit of all the arts, I should even say, for the products of human activity have an aesthetic value precisely insofar as that of which they are signs, their content, is immanent to their form. Now it is only in music that this relation of immanence is found to be realized in all its purity."

like that of music, in which the relation of duration and interval cannot change without the work's ceasing to be itself. In the majority of cases, translating a poem causes the poetry to disappear, unless the translation be itself a new poem in sympathy with the first one—one of those "correspondences" in which the intuitions "respond" to each other. Certain poetic elements, however, lend themselves to translation: the play of images, the intellectual surprise which their juxtaposition arouses, a certain wit, even though the inspiration be tragic, a certain superior and refined "amusement," can pass from one language to another by means of a work of adaptation which does not harm the poetry. Even that kind of poetry which depends on the poignant beauty of a certain quality of intuition and of sentiment, found for example in an Henri Michaux, that poetry also is translatable, though not without some damage . . .

We have said that in poetry the words are at the same time objects and signs, and first of all objects: let us add at once that while being primarily objects (object-images), they still remain, and are more than ever signs, and, this time, in their very quality of objects constituting the matter of the poem. Why is this so? Because, of itself, poetry does not consist of a material object turned in upon itself, but refers to the universality of beauty and of being, perceived each time, it is true, in an individual existence. But it is by our spiritual and intuitive powers that we refer to being. The words which the poet uses cannot be stripped of their role as signs without depriving the poetry of its essential ties with transcendental beauty. It is not in order to communicate ideas, it is to maintain contact with the universe of intuitiveness that they must thus remain signs. As signs, the words also refer us to all that psychological complexity into which the poet proposes—instinctively—to make us enter, and which he needs to express after his manner, that is to say in a determinate form (and, if the poem is beautiful, in a necessary form). It follows from all this that if one reduces completely the words' function as signs, one enfeebles the poem's power of communication and of domination—at the last extreme one annihilates the poetic sense itself, which is spirit. Thus we can understand why, although logical sense cannot be required in poetry for its own sake, for the sake of clarity of reason, still logical non-sense voluntarily and systematically imposed is incompatible with poetry. So it is that a certain intelligible signification is necessary even for entry into mystery and the unknown. "It is a fact of experience that the feeling for the unknown is not propagated except as beginning from the known," Marcel Raymond has very truly written.[2] And this is without counting the fact that the word, even reduced to its role of image, is already laden with intelligence and spirit: "The image," it has been said, "is only a magical form of the principle of identity."[3] There is a great deal of truth in this formula.

* * *

An unexpected proof of this obscure and secret connection between poetic sense and intelligible sense was given us one day by a curious observation. A poet, a true poet, was giving a lecture on poetry and reading poems of different authors. The lecturer himself was akin to the poets of obscurity, even of non-sense, and especially to Lautréamont. He detested logic in poetry—for quite legitimate reasons; he could not even bear a too highly accentuated aid from rhythm and rime, in which he saw a kind of fabrication, as well as an unfair attempt at seduction. Sensitive and rebellious, he was angry at words, forged new words with the hammer of his anger.

[2] *De Baudelaire au Surréalisme.*

[3] Pierre Guéguen, *Nouvelles Littéraires,* 1 June, 1929.

And so it happened that he read a poem whose intelligible sense revealed itself quite ingenuously, whose beauty he valued, a poem written by a poet whom he loved—and since he liked neither the intelligibility nor the music of poetry, he massacred the poem, because in reading it he instinctively (and also voluntarily) deprived it of all intonation; he read it without accent, in an inhuman manner. And the beautiful poem was stripped of its beauty, it died; the reader had caused it to lose its poetic sense in depriving it of its aura of intelligible signification.

But when he read some other pages, quite close to non-sense, certain texts all charged with a thick and consubstantial obscurity, he lent himself so well to the generating sentiment of these texts that he did not commit a single error in his desire to make the full poetic resonance of them felt. Now here is what seemed to me very remarkable—that in magnifying the poetic sense as he did, he was obliged to read them (and he did it instinctively) in a manner which gave them an appearance of logical sense. By an intonation full of suggestion, by a rhythmic gesticulation, by a certain ordered manner throughout all that long reading, he gave an apparent signification to texts which were quite free of all logical connection, a signification which depended here entirely on the rhythm, the delivery, and on the sensitivity and intelligence of the reader. In short, the reader played here the role of the intelligence in dreams. Although bound by sleep (and that is why the principle of non-contradiction appears to be abolished), the intelligence does not sleep, it penetrates, it surrounds the most incoherent series of images with a mysterious atmosphere of clarity . . .

One can make a complementary experiment by reading a poem lacking all apparent intelligibility without in any way supplementing the non-sense which it claims to be. Read thus, the text will be reduced to a *quantity* of words without qualitative connection among them, that is to say, empty of all poetic sense.

We may add that it will almost always be unjust to read in this manner even the most obscure of poems, if poem there be. Because the generating sentiment of the poetic work has a very determinate sense for the poet himself (we are not speaking here of automatic writing), to which he relates and adjusts his expression, until the poem comes to resemble that sense, which is in itself ineffable. And the poet cannot do that without the aid of the intelligence, however instinctively, in however shadowy a fashion it may act. He will write even his non-senses with a certain secret measure, a certain music; in spite of everything, in spite of himself, he will write with a rhythm of phrase which, if the reader observe it, will give to the poem, at least by intonation, an appearance and even more than an appearance of sense, an intelligible resonance. It is in this sense that we said at the beginning that in one degree or another, in one manner or another, the intelligible sense is always there, making at least an implicit and insidious appeal to the attention of the intelligence.

* * *

Why is this so? Because poetry is a human thing. It is born in man in his deepest self, there where all his faculties originate. When it is exteriorized in an object, in a song, in a poem, it must bear the trace of its origin. If the poet, imbued with preconceived and systematic ideas, lay hand upon one or another of its roots to pull it up, upon one or another of its features to efface it, he does an impious thing, he wounds the poem in its process of becoming, and poetry flees through these wounds. To reduce poetry to the simple flow of images is just as arbitrary as to tie it to the reasoning reason. To suppress systematically either the intelligible sense, when it presents itself in the poetic intuition itself, or the expression of the sentiments and of sensibility, is to impair the sincerity and the purity of the inspiration just as surely as if one wished to render the poem didactic by dint of clarity. There exists, without a doubt, the legitimate labor of the poet, which follows the intuition and the conception, but he must know how to construct his work without denaturing anything. No doubt some transposition is necessary, but it is given with the poetic inspiration itself, it is not done afterwards, it is the spontaneous act of the poet. That which goes further is fabrication. And if some great poet should pretend to reduce poetry to that, it is perhaps out of modesty, irony, or sadness.

When that which has moved and concentrated the poet in a profound—and obscure—experience is in itself a supremely intelligible reality, an unbearable light—even though it result in an obscure knowledge of contact and union, which vibrates with the unspeakable complexity of mystery—the poet will tend involuntarily to express himself with a certain clarity, with a high degree of intelligible sense; we have an eminent example of this in the Psalmist.

But if the poet's emotion results from a reality in itself obscure—"obscure as feeling," as Paul Reverdy puts it—he will tend to express himself according to the obscure mode of his initial emotion, like Reverdy himself.

Is that not what Rimbaud said? "The poet is really a stealer of fire . . . *If what he brings back from over there has form, he gives form; if it is unformed, he gives unformedness.*"[4]

* * *

Song and poetry seek to liberate an experience, a substantial knowledge. As knowledge, it seeks an expression; as

[4] *Lettre du Voyant* (to Paul Demeny, May 15, 1871).

substantial, it is properly speaking ineffable. That is why it is not expressed in the manner of reasoning, nor of a didactic exposition. Born in a vital experience, life itself, it asks to be expressed by life-bearing signs, signs which will conduct the one who receives them back to the ineffability of the original experience. Since in this contact all the sources of our faculties have been touched, the echo of it ought itself also to be total. We do not at all wish to say here that the poetic work ought to be the mirror of our psychic states. The relation of the poet to his work is not so simple as that. It is of the creative sources that we are speaking. Thus Reverdy can say, in the same work,[5] both that "the value of a work exists by reason of the poignant contact of the poet with his destiny," and "that it is no longer a matter of arousing emotion by the more or less pathetic telling of a human-interest story, but as grandly, as purely as it is done in the evening by the sky crackling with stars, by the sea, calm, imposing, tragic, or even a silent drama played by the clouds beneath the sun."

We said a moment ago that to some degree the intelligible sense is always necessary to the poetic sense. Now we are brought back to the other aspect of things, to that obscurity which is also, to some degree, always there. The poetic sense, in short, is not the same as the logical sense, and the poem, born in the obscurity of withdrawal (*recueillement*), is necessarily obscure to some degree, be it only by virtue of "some" instinctive "slip" in the choice of words. Without being incompatible with the intelligible sense, this obscurity subsists in all true poetry, as the soul of the poetry.

But there are all sorts of obscurity. Between the intelligible poetry of a Virgil or a Baudelaire and the non-sense cherished for its own sake in certain surrealist texts, are found all

[5] *Le Gant de Crin,* Paris, Plon (*Le Roseau d'Or*).

degrees of intelligibility and of obscurity. And the causes of this are diverse. Let us try to analyse some of them.

The principal cause of the obscurity which goes to the point of non-sense is truly, even if the poet is an atheist, of a quality which it is impossible not to call religious. A pathetic cause, and one which in our day has erupted with an unprecedented intensity, it is first of all—in Lautréamont, in Rimbaud—the despair of ever seizing absolute reality, the interior life in its pure liberty; and for others, in the early period of surrealism, it was the hope, that suddenly surged up, for the rediscovery of that river of the spirit which flows under all our customary activity, of that profound, authentic reality, foreign to all formulae, perceived in those "minutes of abandonment to hidden forces" which vivify. "To attest that the game is not yet up, that all can perhaps be saved—that is the essential of the surrealist message."[6]

In that natural ecstasy in which our soul re-immerses itself so to speak in its source, and from which it issues renewed and fortified for the vocation which is its own—whether of poetry or of prayer—the surrealists were caught in the snare of an experience which they could not forget; but, being generally opposed to all religious form and even to the idea of God, they wished to seek therein only the sources of poetry, while they burdened poetry with the duties of sanctity—without the means of sanctity, which are essentially the giving of the self. They overwhelmed poetry with this weight, at first. Later, not having obtained from it what they expected, they undervalued it. And then a new despair pushed them toward other spiritual adventures.

From that passive withdrawal into the best part of themselves, which is rare and fecund and which must in some way

[6] Marcel Raymond, *op. cit.*

be deserved, they went on to the passivity of psychological automatism (under the influence of Freud perhaps), of which everyone is capable by the application of the proper techniques. And as for poetry, their error was to believe that its substantial truth is expressed by that psychic automatism, taken as a synonym of the real functioning of thought, and that the image is all-sufficient. But automatism unbinds that which concentration and withdrawal had brought into the unity of life. The liberty so ardently desired presupposes the possession of the self in unity—even though carried away and ravished—not dispersion. "The spirits of the Prophets," says St. Paul, "are subject to the Prophets."[7]

Doubtless automatism voluntarily let loose does not hinder, even facilitates sometimes, the discovery of images, because the imagination is not abolished by automatism (nor by madness). But these discoveries furnish raw and scattered materials, and the procedure in itself has nothing to do with real liberty of spirit. And, even with the surrealist poets, the automatism is not absolute; the memory, unbound by that passivity, brings back to consciousness what the consciousness had known long before, and forgotten. Thus there is no absolutely pure invention here either. And the spirit of revolt and of indignation, a profound pessimism, resentment against men and things, have animated in a very *significative* manner many texts that are voluntarily obscure.

[7] St. Paul, *I Cor.* xiv. 32. "And in order," says John of St. Thomas, "that we should not think that man born of the Spirit is pushed by a furious impulse like those whom an evil spirit possesses, the Lord affirms first of all that the Spirit blows where it listeth, in order to signify that to be born of the Spirit brings, rather than takes away, the liberty of election. Indeed, what merit would remain if the Spirit operated in the will not by inspiring it and balancing its inclination, but by violating it? And that is why the Apostle says that 'the spirits of the prophets are subject to the prophets' (when they employ the prophetic spirit in order to announce hidden things), just the contrary of what takes place in delirious ravings." Jean de S. Thomas, *Les Dons du Saint-Esprit,* French translation, 2nd ed., Paris, Téqui, 1950, p. 3.

In a more simply human and more simply poetic order, it could be shown that a certain obscurity follows on an inspiration which proceeds essentially from sentiment or from dreams, and that, on the other hand, the sense of the unsoundable mystery of things, the revelation, the discovery of unwonted analogies, the desire to express, come what may, the ineffable, are the positive and transcendental causes of the obscurity in poetry—sometimes, as in Claudel, by an excess of intellectual concentration.

Another source of obscurity is found in the extreme necessity of renovating forms. This obscurity is especially inevitable in the inventors who arise after a long period of conformism.

When the poet is confronted with the insufficiency of words, when he seeks sonorities yet unknown, when he wishes to give unique expression to a unique perception, he easily admits obscurity and non-sense and composes new words; or he even tries to create a new language. Then the words created answer especially to exigencies of a musical order in the poet's sensibility. But if the case of the poet then appears to resemble the case of the composer this resemblance remains quite superficial, because with the true composer the work does not escape the control of the spirit, or the necessities of unity and equilibrium, while the poets who create new words by pure instinct obey above all the inclination of their sensibility, if not the spirit of satire or of indignation, and perhaps personal exigencies of transposition.

The case of Joyce is different. His researches have at the same time a plastic and a philological character. He creates new words for thoughts and sensations for which he does not find an expression in the language. Here the non-sense is such for the reader only. In reality, the author writes in a foreign language, known only by himself, but very well known by him.

The non-sense of Mallarmé, on the contrary, is a veritable spoken music (I do not mean to say a song). The pleasure which this music gives is very great. And Mallarmé is very conscious of this "magic." There are musics, and among the most beautiful, which give the impression of being languages. It seems that if one were close enough to the orchestra one could distinguish the words, a whole discourse; but one is never close enough for that, and what reaches us are the vowels without the consonants—it is a magic music which appears to defy us a little. It is the inverse of this which is produced by Mallarmé: one is a little too near to perceive the whole musical development of this orchestrated poetry;[8] one has only the beginnings of it, one hears the separate accents of the instruments—these are words, and they are not words, it is a spoken music—quite the inverse of the musical poetry of Verlaine. Here also the action of the intelligence is present, an intelligence filled, in fact, with occult notions.

* * *

And so we are led, in this way, to the poetry in which intelligibility predominates over obscurity.

There is a clarity which comes of ignorance—there is nothing mysterious for the ignorant man who is unaware of his ignorance—from ignorance also of the nature of poetry

[8] "The whole language [since the death of Victor Hugo] breaks loose according to a free disjunction into a thousand simple elements; and, as I shall indicate, not without similitude with the multiplicity of cries of an orchestration, which remains verbal." Mallarmé, *Divagation Première*.

and of the role of words in poetry. The words are employed in a prosaic manner, that is to say, as simple signs of ideas. And the poet supposes he has acquitted himself in regard to poetry because he has observed some formal rules of versification. Thus it is with didactic poetry, and with a certain neoclassicism.

There is a clarity which comes of naïveté, when this is united with great gifts of imagination and simple sentiments. This is especially characteristic of folk poetry.

Another sort of clarity results from the abundance of philosophical and religious ideas united to poetic genius, and from the profundity of their invisceration in the soul. As we noted a moment ago, however, the very richness of this philosophical and religious effort, and the super-abundance of sense itself, can produce obscurity.

Finally, it must be recognized that up to the present, clarity has characterized great mastery, magnificent mastery, that of Homer, of Virgil, of Dante, of Shakespeare, of Racine, of Goethe, of Pushkin, of Baudelaire . . .

The poetic gift is so powerful in them that it consumes and brings to the state of fusion the most resistant materials: the clear and precise knowledges, the most prosaic necessities of the language. Everything burns with these "ravishers of fire," and everything takes the form which the good pleasure of Poetry wishes. Here we find at the same time unheard-of discoveries, and poetry, the light of intuition, and that of intelligence. And this poetry persuades us that the mystery of the sun and of radiant daylight is not less than that of the obscurest night.

* * *

We believe then that a certain intelligibility, like a certain obscurity, subsists in every true poetic work. Intelligibility, obscurity, mark the origin of the work conceived in those depths of the soul where intelligence and desire, intuition and sensibility, imagination and love have their common source . . . Once it begins to emerge from this generative and nourishing center, the work appeals, each time in a different fashion, to those powers of the soul, each of which has its own manner of attaining to the real and expressing it.

The source of poetry and of all creative intuition is in a certain experience which one can call an obscure and savory "knowledge," with a thoroughly spiritual savor,[9] for at these

[9] We read in *Mesures* (15 April, 1938) an article by René Daumal, which is of the greatest interest in relation to Hindu poetics. It is moving to find in the Sanskrit texts of the Vedic period this definition of poetry: *"Poetry is a word of which the Savor is the essence."* If the word proffered by the Poet, has Savor for its essence, it is that the poetic experience, from which this word emanates, is itself a savory knowledge. We say that this savor is entirely spiritual. The Vedic texts say that it is "supernatural, supra-physical" or "unworldly." Thus savor is one of the principal characters of analogy between Poetry and the Mystical Experience. For savor, which seems to be connected with every knowledge by affective connaturality, pertains also to the most elevated of the Gifts of the Holy Spirit, to the Gift of Wisdom, which communicates a savory science, with a properly supernatural savor (Cf. Jean de S. Thomas, *Les Dons du Saint-Esprit,* French trans. by R. Maritain, Paris, Téqui, 1950).

The essence of poetry, M. Daumal continues, possesses certain virtues by which it manifests itself: *Suavity,* that is "a refreshment born of the liquefaction of the spirit;" *Ardor,* that is, "an expansive kindling of the spirit;" *Evidence:* "that which penetrates the spirit with the rapidity of fire in dry wood is Evidence, present with all the savors . . . This third virtue of the savor . . . has as its function *to cause to understand,* while the other two have as a function *to cause to feel"* . . . But Poetry does not cause one to understand in the manner of prose; "prose speaks of something, poetry *makes* something with words." The poetic sense is not the "literal" sense but the "suggested" sense. "The term *resonance* (Dhvani) is more especially reserved" to this form of signification.

"The suggested sense is different from the literal sense [and as well from the figurative sense]:

"In relation to the auditor, in that the literal sense is perceptible by the simple grammarian, while the suggested sense will not be perceived except by conscious *experience*. . . ; in relation to *the means of apprehension,* in that

depths all is spirit and life, and every poet knows that he penetrates there by a concentration of all his senses into unity, however fleeting it be—and that this is a primary condition of poetic conception. We are taking concentration here in the passive sense of *quietude,* not in the sense of voluntary and active concentration.

This concentration or withdrawal is the first gift which is made to the poet, and it is also a natural disposition which must be cultivated. It is because of this, it is in this sense, I suppose, that Rimbaud wrote: "The first study of the man who wishes to be a poet is knowledge of himself, entire. He seeks his soul, he inspects it, he tries it, learns it."[10]

---

the literal sense is communicated by the pronouncing of the words (the auditor being passive), whereas the suggested sense will not be seized except by the activity of an exercised intelligence; in relation to the *effect,* in that the literal sense gives only information, whereas the suggested sense provokes Admiration (therefore the enjoyment of the Savor) . . ."

Thus the exigency of the (suggested) sense is rigorous. "Incomplete sense depreciates the Savor." Only intentional non-senses, those deriving from poetic style, are allowable, such as: "The bird Tchakora drinks the rays of the moon . . ."

Answering to all exigencies, "a single word, it is said, when well used and well understood, is the Cow from which may be milked all the desires of this world and of heaven."

The Hindu poetics thus appears to leave less place than ours to a certain obscurity. It would admit Racine much more easily than Mallarmé. This is because for Hindu thought poetry has an essentially ministerial function, having to do with Wisdom and with the supreme contemplative Deliverance. It seems, indeed, that the Vedic books, while making an eminent place for Poetry, consider it above all as a way and a means: "Poetry is a means of aiding our deficient reason to accede to the unveiled teaching of the truth." Thus it is necessary that the Poet should already have taken several steps on the road of this teaching, since his task is to attract us "by offering us a tidbit, a savor to taste."

The value of the poetic experience in itself and of the ends of poetry in its own sphere, leaving aside the legitimate subordinaton of all ends to the final end, does not appear to have been disengaged by Hindu thought and appreciated for itself. That, we believe, is a privilege of the Occident, and of modern times. In a general way one can say that in India the predominant preoccupation with Salvation attracted and absorbed poetry, like philosophy, in theological finalities.

[10] *Lettre du Voyant.*

This withdrawal is a psychological phenomenon *analogically* common to the poetic state and to mystical contemplation. The same is true for the obscure and savory knowledge which accompanies it. It is the resemblance between these states which makes Jean Royère say: "Poetry . . . is religious. Its essential obscurity comes from its being the history of a soul and its wishing to observe the mystery; but this obscurity is luminous . . ."[11] (A curious recollection of the *et nox illuminatio mea in deliciis meis* of Psalm 138.) Robert Desnos does not believe in God, but he in turn writes: ". . . no one has a more religious spirit than I. . . ."[12] But this is also what made Henri Bremond say, wrongly we believe, that "the poetic activity is a natural and profane approximation of mystical activity. . . , a confused and maladroit approximation, full of holes and blanks, so much so that the poet indeed is only an evanescent mystic or a mystic *manqué*."[13] There are several confusions in all this, it seems to me. And first of all, it is proper to protest in the name of poetry: poetry is not something *manqué;* to say that it is a mysticism *manqué* is to do it too much and not enough honor. It is not mysticism; it is a particular essence, a being which has its own nature; it has its own origins and its own ontological laws. In the second place, it must be considered that the sort of obscure knowledge or affective experience which is that of poetry does not touch the common source of all that exists in the same manner as does the obscure knowledge of the mystical experience. *All sources are in Thee* . . . Here, in the mystical experience, the object touched is the uncreated Abysm, God the savior and vivifier, known obscurely as present and united with the soul of him who contemplates; while the obscure knowledge which is

[11] *La Phalange,* 1909.
[12] *Revue Européenne,* March, 1924.
[13] *Prière et Poésie,* p. 208.

that of the Poet, and which touches, as object known, the things and the reality of the word rather than God himself, flows from a union of another order, more or less intense, with God the creator and organizer of nature.

Every great vocation confers, on him who is called, the capacity for a certain union with God, through a particular relation to Him, whose essence transcends the multiplicity of his attributes; and the well-defined vocations are distinguished among themselves by pertaining to one or the other of the divine attributes into which the supreme Simplicity is divided in the eyes of the created intelligence.

Poets and other artists, the great inventors and the saints, all draw on the same divine source, but with different dispositions, and according to essentially distinct types of relation to that source. They are all of them imitators of God, but some are specially called to augment the human treasure of beauty and science—they are imitators of God the creator; the others are specially called to enter into the mystery of the Deity itself and to make known in the world, by some image, by some resemblance, the Sanctity of God, in imitation of Jesus Christ, by abnegation of self and of all that is of this world. Nature and grace have qualified workers, who render a mysterious mutual assistance to one another for the raising and spiritualization of humanity. It is quite properly then that the former are called "creators" and the latter "saints."

The results which follow on these diverse callings, these experiences distinct in essence in spite of their proximity in the same divine source, are, like the callings, quite different, for the poet and for the contemplative. Every time that there is natural or supernatural contemplation, the contemplation is itself its own fruit and its own resting-place; and in mystical contemplation properly so called the obscure and savory knowledge attained tends to overflow in immanent acts. In the poetic experience, on the other hand, the obscure experience, if it attains a high degree of intensity, tends to fructify in an object. Thus the poet, returning from his withdrawal into himself, will write a poem; but the mystic, moved, stirred by his God, will intensify his contemplative life (rather it will be intensified in him), and the acts of the virtues and gifts which join him to God: he will love God and men more deeply. The poet finds the plenitude of his joy in *realizing* his inspiration in the creation of a new form. But for him who comes back to the surface of life from the depth of mystical union, it is affliction to become conscious again of images and distinct forms. The feeling of plenitude for the mystics is in the repose of union, of adhesion to God: *Mihi autem adhaerere Deo bonum est.* The poet, on the other hand, would find perfect joy in the adequacy of the created form to the creative inspiration.

* * *

But if the mystic is at the same time a poet, what will be in him the existential relations of the poetic gifts and the mystical gifts? It would be a good and useful thing to be able to penetrate this mystery of life. It is in any case certain that these diverse gifts furnish a favorable climate to one another. At the moment when that binding of the powers of the soul which is characteristic of the mystical experience is relaxed, and the mystical concentration or withdrawal is about to terminate, it often happens that it gives way to poetic activity; and that ought not to surprise us, since the whole soul is enlivened by union with God. This is seen clearly in the case of the holy prophets, Moses, Isaiah, David, and the others; and in the case of the great contemplatives like Seuss, Ruysbroeck, Theresa of Avila, John of the Cross, to cite only well-known names. Contemplation does not necessarily produce poets, but these great mystics were also poets, whom the experience of divine things had exalted. According to the multitude of their gifts they have had the power of communicating to us a little of their ineffable experience.

But it also happens that the poet passes from poetic withdrawal to mystical withdrawal. This passage is doubtless accomplished by the agency of a certain enthusiasm and a certain passivity of spirit which renders the poet more apt to receive the divine impressions. The Bible offers us an example of this kind in the Second Book of Kings, and St. Thomas refers to it in the *Summa Theologica*:[14] "Jehosaphat having inquired of Elisha concerning the future, and the spirit of prophecy having failed him, Elisha had a harp-player brought in. *And while this man sang to the harp the hand of Jehovah was upon Elisha and he said: Thus saith the Lord . . .*"[15] It seems then that the spirit of the Prophet was favorably disposed by the music and poetry to receive the light of God, present but invisible to the distraught and divided soul. And what is true of prophecy can also be true of contemplation.

The fact is that when the poet passes from the state of poetic withdrawal, the source of images and forms, to the mystical sleep, images and forms are lost, drunk up by the silence of the soul as rain is drunk up by the sea. The poet has perhaps lost his poem, but in the scale of absolute values that is an inestimable gain.

It is, then, the habit of a certain withdrawal, of a certain sleep of the faculties, of a certain interior silence, which disposes the poet sometimes to divine influences, sometimes to the keen perception of natural causes: "When the soul is abstracted from the sense," says St. Thomas, "it becomes more apt to receive the influence of spiritual substances and

[14] *Sum. Theol.*, II-II, 171, a, 2, s. c.
[15] II Kings, III, 15.

also to follow the subtle movements which are born in the imagination from the impression of natural causes, something which is very difficult when it is absorbed by sensible things."[16]

One sees in this way how serious it would be for a poet not to have for poetry a respect which is sacred, for him to let his gifts be contaminated by any impurity; not only would art thus be turned aside from its proper ends, but also the poet would be prevented from acceding to the contemplative state—which ought to be much more frequently enjoyed by him than it is, and toward which, as we have just seen, he is naturally disposed.[17] For every elevated nature there is moreover a law of transcendance which alone assures the stability of perfection. Goethe has given an admirable formulation of it: "Everything that is perfect in its species," he says, "must rise above its species, become something else, an incomparable being."

These vital relations between the mystical order and the poetic order still leave intact, however, the real distinctness of their essence. On a general level, in the order of mystical contemplation, it is a matter above all of knowing and loving —of knowing *in order to* love. No doubt in the case of poetry a certain knowledge of the created world and of the enigmatic relations among beings is involved, but all this knowledge, which is a knowledge by connaturality, does not tend of itself towards love; it tends toward the creation of beautiful works, in the case of the poet toward the making of a work in words;

[16] *Sum. Theol.*, II-II, 172, I, ad. I. "Poetry," writes Jean Cocteau, "predisposes, then, to the supernatural. The hyper-sensible atmosphere in which it envelopes us sharpens our secret senses, and our antennae plunge into depths of which our official senses are ignorant." *Le Rappel à Ordre,* Paris, Stock, 1926, p. 219.

[17] "The only true source of art is in our hearts, the language of a pure and candid soul . . ." says C. D. Friedrich, the painter and poet of the finest epoch of German romanticism. "Every authentic work is conceived in a sacred hour, born in a blessed hour; an interior impulsion creates it, often without the artist's knowing."

and these words are interrelated in such a way that they act, as the flute moved to sound by the breath, like an instrument of the poetic state. Thus the poem is a vehicle of poetic inspiration as the flute is a vehicle of music, the painter's brush a vehicle of vision.[18]

Poetry is the fruit of a contact of the spirit with reality, which is in itself ineffable, and with the source of reality, which we believe to be God himself in that movement of love which causes him to create images of his beauty. That which is thus conceived in the mysterious retreats of being is expressed with a certain savory illogic, which is not non-sense but a superabundance of sense.

Song, poetry in all its forms, seeks, as we said above, to liberate a substantial experience. (And perhaps also, because of that, the life of a saint is Poetry . . .)

The brooding repose which is provided by such an experience acts as a refreshing bath, a rejuvenation and purification of the spirit. Is that the secret principle of Aristotelian catharsis? We cannot esteem too highly the profundity of the quiet which all our faculties then enjoy. It is a concentration of all the energies of the soul, but a peaceful, tranquil concentration, which involves no tension; the soul enters into its repose, in this place of refreshment and of peace superior to any feeling.[19] It dies "the death of the Angels," but only to

[18] "Poetry is the attempt to represent, or to reconstitute by means of articulated language, those things or that thing which cries, tears, caresses, kisses, sighs, etc., try obscurely to express, and which certain objects in which there is an appearance of life or of supposed design seem to wish to express." Paul Valéry.

[19] We read in *Mesures* (15 July 1937) a study of Heidegger on Hölderlin in which we find a remarkable confirmation of the reflections offered here: "In poetry," says Heidegger, explaining the thought of Hölderlin, "man is concentrated upon the depth of his human reality. In it he accedes to quietude; not at all, it is true, to the illusory quietude of inactivity and emptiness of thought, but to that infinite quietude in which all the energies are mutually in action."

revive in exaltation and enthusiasm, in that state which is wrongly called "inspiration," because inspiration was nothing other, indeed, than this very repose itself, in which it escaped from sight. Now the mind, reinvigorated and enlivened, enters into a happy activity, so easy that everything seems to be given to it at once and, as it were, from outside. In reality, everything was there, in the shadow, hidden in the spirit and in the blood; everything that is going to be manifested in operation was there, but we knew it not. We knew neither how to discover it nor how to make use of it before having re-immersed ourselves in those tranquil depths.

Such is, we believe, the source of poetic sense, in itself free and self-sufficient, and of what it inevitably brings with it in the way of logical *sense* and, at the same time, *non-sense.*

RAÏSSA MARITAIN

Magic, Poetry, and Mysticism

WE REGRET NOT TO HAVE BEEN ACQUAINTED, BEFORE WRITING our study "Sense and Non-Sense in Poetry," with the important works which Albert Béguin has devoted to the romantic poets. The two volumes which treat of "The Romantic Soul and the Dream," and the essay on "Gérard de Nerval" followed by "Poetry and Mysticism" illustrate and corroborate in so significant a manner several of the views presented in this little book that we should like in connection with them to take up again and complete several of the points treated in our study.

In "Poetry and Mysticism," Albert Béguin writes that "the aesthetics which has been elaborated through symbolism and surrealism . . . clearly attributes to art an efficacy which is quite close to that which one recognizes in magical powers, in mystical efforts, and in the contemplations of the speculative intellect."

We think, and we have tried to show, that poetry is distinct in nature from mysticism, and that the kind of knowledge which belongs to it, affective knowledge, turned toward the creation of a new object, is also distinct from speculative knowledge, which is objective union with the reality known.

I shall return later to the question of the relations between poetry and mysticism; I should like first to say a few words about the relation between "magical powers" and poetry.

The search for magical powers has been a perpetual temptation for poets: a fallacious seduction which has caused those whom it has led into its blind alley to lose first of all the disinterestedness essential to any activity of the spirit, and then the very taste for poetic creation. Of this temptation a Gérard de Nerval was so conscious that he was determined to triumph over it "by an admirable effort of will;"[1] a temptation which Rimbaud finally escaped, but at what a price—by renouncing poetry itself: no doubt "because it was evil," . . . "this ambition to conquer exceptional powers," but also, one may believe, because of the discouraging clarity with which he rapidly saw that poetry does not confer such powers. Nevertheless, indefatigably, in spite of all the disappointments, poets return to their search. What is it that they seek, precisely? What are the "powers" so ardently coveted? They would like to force the gates of the mystery which penetrates us and envelopes us on all sides and to create beings, or act upon created beings, by efficacious signs, as if by sorcery. And to do that, in some cases, by a science of the arrangements of letters and words in accordance with the teaching of the Cabala. For Mallarmé, the most efficacious of these arrangements is the poem.

But the gates of mystery cannot be forced; it is necessary to give oneself in order to enter into the house of God or that of the devil. There is no other recipe; and even so, one is not always sure of being received.

As for the fabrication of a poem in the capacity of a charm, according to some occult science, that is a questionable kind

[1] A. Béguin, *Gérard de Nerval,* Paris, Stock, 1936.

of sorcery; in any case it has but little to do with the ways of knowledge, of wisdom and of beauty. May we not acknowledge how much of poetry a great poet like Mallarmé lost in his desperate calculations, and that for no efficacious magic, for no secret science to be left to the poets his successors. Such a misfortune did not occur to Baudelaire, nor to Edgar Allan Poe, because they wished to know no other alchemy than that which is in the service of poetry itself.

Poe, however, believed in the "power of the word." He even gave this title to one of his stories, and M. Roland de Renéville sees in that a very important testimony in favor of the magical powers of poetry: "Edgar Poe," he writes, "did not fail to reveal the knowledge he had of the occult possibilities of language. In the story entitled 'The Power of Words,' he refers to 'a true philosophy' to affirm that all movement is creative, that the source of all movement is thought, that, finally, the source of all thought is God."[2] Does the poet not make the two "spirits" of his dialogue discuss the material power of the word?

OINOS. But why, Agathos, do you weep—and why, oh why do your wings droop as we hover above this fair star—which is the greenest and yet most terrible of all we have encountered in our flight? Its brilliant flowers look like a fair dream—but its fierce volcanoes like the passions of a turbulent heart.

AGATHOS. They *are*!—they *are*! This wild star—it is now three centuries since, with clasped hands, and with streaming eyes, at the feet of my beloved—I spoke it—with a few passionate sentences—into birth. Its brilliant flowers *are* the dearest of all unfulfilled dreams, and its raging volcanoes *are* the passions of the most turbulent and unhallowed of hearts.

Well then, does this text really refer to a magical conception of poetry and of the word? I do not believe so. What

[2] Roland de Renéville, *L'Expérience Poétique,* Paris, Gallimard, 1938.

we have to do with here, as in *Eureka,* is a pantheistic philosophy and cosmology, in which all movement and every action participate in the efficacy of a divine action, the effects of which, however, are no more knowable to us than the divine essence itself. Actually, it is after death that the disincarnated personages of Poe's dialogue discover the creative effects—which answer to no design premeditated by them—of words expressing their terrestrial "dreams" and "passions." I hardly see a place in Poe's cosmology for researches leading to magical formulae. And still less in his poetry, which was always perfectly free of any anxiety of this order, and of which he would never have wished to make an instrument of "power." Poe was a perfectly disinterested spirit, he was glad of a discovery which gave him, he believed, a true knowledge of the universe; and it is in its beauty, not in some efficacy or other, that he saw the proof of its verity. "To the few who love me and whom I love," he says in the dedication of *Eureka,* "to those who feel rather than to those who think—to the dreamers and those who put faith in dreams as in the only realities—I offer this Book of Truths, not in its character of Truth-Teller, but for the Beauty that abounds in its Truth [Baudelaire and Poe still dare to use these capital letters]; constituting it true."

To affirm the efficacy, infinitely reverberated—up to "the throne of the Divinity," as Poe says—of the least spiritual movement and of the least spiritual act, in no wise engages one in the ways of magic. It is an attitude which justifies itself in the eyes of the scientist, as of the poet and the mystic. Following Poe and Baudelaire, we can cite Léon Bloy, who loved them so much: "A given movement of Grace, which saves me from a grave peril, could have been determined by a given act of love accomplished this morning or five hundred years ago by a very obscure man whose soul corresponded mysteriously to mine, and who thus received his reward. . . What one calls free will is like those common flowers whose winged seeds are carried by the wind, enormous distances sometimes, and in all directions, to plant one knows not what mountains or what valleys. The revelation of these prodigies will be the spectacle of a minute which will last for eternity."[3] And again, in *Le Désespéré*: "Every man who produces a free act projects his personality to the infinite. If he gives a coin to a poor man ungraciously, that coin pierces the hand of the poor man, falls, pierces the earth, bores holes in the suns, traverses the firmament, and compromises the universe. If he commits an impure act, perhaps he darkens thousands of hearts that he does not know, that correspond mysteriously to him and that have need that that man be pure, as a traveller dying of thirst needs the glass of the water mentioned in the Gospel. A charitable act, a movement of true pity, sings divine praises in his name, from Adam to the end of the ages, it cures the sick, consoles the desperate, appeases the tempests, ransoms the captives, converts the infidels, and protects the human race."

In its pure line poetry has no magic power other than that of "charming" and seducing, of "enchanting" and moving, of taming hearts, of communicating to them the appeals and presences, and all that experience of the world and all that hidden reality which the poet himself has experienced.[4] Beyond that, in the line of "powers," it is no longer poetry but conniving with forces that are suspect and in the end disappointing as a lie. But in the immaculate line of its

[3] *Méditations d'un Solitaire,* Paris, Mercure de France.

[4] Cf. Jacques Maritain, "Signe et Symbole," *Revue Thomiste,* April, 1938. (*Quatre Essais sur l'Esprit,* 1939)—"It is, it seems, by virtue of such a slipping that the primitives and the partisans of poetry-magic confound the *presence of cognoscibility* of the signified in the sign with a *physical presence* and an operative efficacy."

own experience Poetry has exceedingly more important powers. Through it the poet learns that way which "goes toward the interior" of which Novalis speaks, and he thus approaches, more or less, ultimate Reality.

For the poet as for the mystic, all avaricious research is a grave fault which scares away the Gifts. But he who has received them and keeps them in a disinterested heart receives in his turn the grace of giving, and he abounds in generous works, the only power the ambition for which causes neither the poet nor the saint to fall. The German and French romantics and the surrealists tried more or less innocently to seek for magical powers. It was sometimes "the hope of an absolute knowledge which for them would be more and better than a simple 'knowledge': an 'unlimited power,' the magical instrument of a redemption of nature."[5] And sometimes it was the desire to remake the world, which disappointed them, according to their own wish. But "since we could not, in order to equal God, become creators," writes Moritz in his *Journal of a Visionary*,[6] "we made ourselves destroyers, we created backwards, since we could not create in the direction of the future. We made for ourselves a universe of destruction, and then, with a tender complacency, we contemplated our work in history, in tragedy, and in our poems." A singular prescience. . . . At the origin of such a deviation, however, there is the dazzlement of a real experience, in the heart of man, of that which surpasses man. We have said that poetic knowledge does not in itself tend toward love, any more, for that matter, than scientific knowledge; but it must be added that all knowledge which is not finally turned toward loving is by that very fact a source of death. Thus the poet in whom

[5] A. Béguin, *L'Ame Romantique et le Rêve,* Marseille, éditions des Cahiers du Sud, 1937.

[6] Quoted by A. Béguin, *ibid.*

there does not arise the enthusiasm and the passionate desire "to rejoin the essential unity . . . as well in the contemplation of the exterior spectacle as in the apprehension of the obscure data of the interior world," gives way almost necessarily, says G. H. von Schubert, "to another movement similar to that which drags man into the abyss. Like Phaeton, the capricious egoism of man wants to possess itself of the chariot of God: he has wished to create for himself that interior enthusiasm which God alone can create."

POETRY AND MYSTICISM

To divert the poetic experience or the mystical experience towards oneself is to offend the heart of God and of things and cause all real substance to vanish in illusion. But when the poet renounces the vain search after magical powers and is willing to submit "to that orientation of his entire being towards a reality which surpasses exterior reality" from which precisely, according to Albert Béguin, recent poetry has received its distinctive character, he enters into true mysteries, and advances in the fruitful and non-deceptive line of his own discoveries. I shall quote a fine page from Albert Béguin which seems to me to describe felicitously the poetic enterprise:

"If the poet abandons himself to this double flow of images, those which come to him from the surrounding spectacle deprive the sensible world of its reality, through a kind of dizziness, render it transparent, assimilate it to a system of symbols which mean more than themselves . . .[7]

Indeed it is difficult with the experience so described to

[7] "The originals of the images and forms which the language of dreams, poetry, and prophecy employs are found in the Nature which surrounds us and which appears to us like a world of Dream incarnate: like a prophetic language whose hieroglyphs were beings and forms." G. H. von Schubert, quoted in *L'Ame Romantique*, I, 206.

know whether it is the most mystical of poetic graces, or the most poetic of mystical graces. Not that we have here a first undifferentiated moment from which the two ways, the poetic and the mystic, would open out; but there are, at this level, two experiences so close to each other (I do not mean that they are always given together, quite the contrary) that there is hardly an idiom which will suffice to differentiate them. But what follows quite naturally from the one or the other reveals the nature of the starting point.

However that may be, the whole of the text which we are citing clearly concerns the poetic experience. And one could hardly insist too much on the importance, in a way infinite, of the intuition which thus reveals to the poet the significative value of things, become communicative of more than they themselves are:

"And the other [images], those which arise from the depths of the being and finally come to correspond with these symbols, compose with them a song which speaks of a realm beyond the real, evoke the paradise of the primitive union, and remind the soul of its mysterious relations." This song which without yet being formulated is composed in the depths of the soul, and which demands to come out later, to be sung—here we recognize the poetic experience properly so called, oriented from the beginning towards expression. "At the height of the poetic experience the frontiers between an exterior and an interior world disappear; all is image, offered to the free disposition of a spirit which recomposes according to its own wish the order of everything given. The poet re-makes from what is given him a universe suiting his own exigencies, according to his pleasure, conforming himself only to the laws of that euphoria which is aroused in him by this rhythm, that sonorous echo, that associaton of forms and colors." Here the poet is in his own realm, here all is submitted to his laws, here he can never be too ambitious; here he can be 'a true god,' if he is Baudelaire . . .[8]

"But, at this sovereign point, the spirit ceases to consider itself as the author of the song in which it finds its felicity; it seems to perceive a voice which is no longer its own. That which speaks is not itself but another *who stirs in the depths,* in a symphony which responds to the stroke of its bow." It is thus that every true poet goes—by his own experience of those depths where, as we noted above, all is spirit and life—from the visible to the invisible, and from images of the real to the reality without images, from which he returns, however, with words, sounds, forms, and colors.

Thus the question naturally arises concerning the relations between Poetry and Mysticism. As to their resemblance and their essential distinction, I have already explained what seems to me to be true; I should like to bring up again here the points of convergence which particularly strike me between M. Albert Béguin's conclusions and my own.

"Call to unity—descent into the regions where the self is renounced in favor of a presence which it perceives within itself—efficacious action of the image: one cannot help, in the first place, noticing singular resemblances between these definitions and those which it is possible to give of the mystical experience."

It is true, the mystic also thirsts for unity and union: unity of all his faculties in peace, union of all his being with God. He too, he especially, frequents "the road which goes toward the interior," up to those mysterious sources where he finds a God more intimate to him than himself. He also feels the need of images, in the meditation which precedes contemplation. And when he finds himself again among us, it is rare that he does not, under the pressure of the abundance of his

[8] Rimbaud, *Lettre du Voyant.*

riches, experience the need of using song and the spoken word to try to communicate the ineffable, to announce to all the presence of God and his goodness—*in aeternum cantabo!* But is the resemblance so perfect that "every boundary between mysticism and poetry must be effaced, and the latter be made the privileged vessel of spiritual ambitions? It is strange, if poetry and mysticism are indistinguishable . . . that all the poets should have the feeling of that *great defeat which perpetuates itself* and of which Aragon once spoke."

Such a feeling, quite different from a simple experience of the internal limitations of art, is it true that *all poets* necessarily experience it? It doubtless occurs the more frequently as the consciousness which poetry acquires of itself turns increasingly to the pure, unlimited desire for poetic knowledge, with which other hopes of the spirit come almost inevitably to be mixed. This feeling of disappointment, in any case, appears to be a distinctive characteristic of essential importance, and sufficient to show, even if it were the only thing, that poetry is not mysticism, and that the poet is preparing bitter disappointments for himself if he demands of Poetry that plenitude of spiritual knowledge which is found at the end of the ascetic and mystic ways. The mystics have never spoken of "that great defeat." It is because they have experimental knowledge, more or less frequent, more or less profound, of that union with God which approaches the perfect Unity. There is the source of their joy; outside of that nothing matters to them (at least for themselves), "outside of that is extreme misery," as one of them, Gerlac Peters, has put it. Whatever otherwise are the trials of barrenness and denudation, the frightful nights that the soul traverses in the quest for union, even at the height of suffering it is never disappointed, provided that it has to do with God and not with men. The plenitude of peace in the mystic, whether it be triumphant or subjacent to terrible combats, proves that he is not mistaken in proposing to attain Unity by the ways of sanctity. If Poetry fulfilled our desires to this degree there would be no "defeat that perpetuates itself;" nor would there be if one did not demand of poetry that it go up to the end of a way where, in any case, it cannot arrive alone. The error, here, witnesses moreover to the grandeur of Poetry, it is the proof of the kinship in the same divine source of the experience of the poet and that of the mystic. But all that poets and mystics have taught us about these things permits us to say, we believe, as we have done above,[9] that if they draw from the same source, it is, however, with different dispositions, and according to essentially distinct types of relation to that Source.

In the exemplary case of a Rimbaud or a Gérard de Nerval, there is more of philosophical error than of pride. But it is an error so dearly paid for that they believed themselves chastised for their audacity and finally retired into silence or remorse. In such a case "the final silence of the poet is a silence of the vanquished one who is resigned; that of the mystics is the peace of him who has achieved the goal of his adventure."[10] No, the resemblance between mysticism and poetry is not an identity; it does not efface their frontiers, though those frontiers are incessantly traversed (especially in the order of natural mysticism) by currents in one direction and the other.

After having insisted on the resemblances, M. Roland de Renéville, in the important book which he has recently published on *The Poetic Experience*, adds with force: "All the same, so many accords, so many coincidences, must give way before the unique [unique it is not, according to our opinion]

[9] *Sense and Non-Sense in Poetry*, pp. 19-21.

[10] A. Béguin, "Poésie et Mystique," annex to *Gérard de Nerval.*

but fundamental difference which separates the poetic experience from the mystical experience: *while the poet progresses toward the Word, the mystic tends toward Silence.* The poet identifies himself with the forces of the manifest universe, while the mystic traverses them and tries to unite with the immutable and unlimited power of the absolute behind them."

Although it very often happens that the mystic feels the need of describing his experience, the fact remains that for him the expression is not a means of completing the experience, is in no way necessary to its conclusion and perfection; it is only a result of superabundance, a generous attempt at communication.

For the poet, on the contrary, the expression is a vital part of his experience, and as it were the fruit of that experience. As Jacques Maritain shows below, "poetic knowledge, which is at the minimum of knowledge but at the maximum of germinative virtuality . . . will only be completely objectified in the work;" and although there can be a poetic experience without a poem, "there is no poetic experience without the secret germ of a poem, however tiny it be." "The necessity of form," says Albert Béguin, "cannot be an accessory or secondary thing in poetry; and that is to say that the realm of poetry, of art, never coincides perfectly with that of mysticism . . . Whatever value one attributes to the poetic act, it remains an act submitted to the necessity of form . . . It ends at the word, and even though convinced that the word has no meaning except by allusion to the Night he has glimpsed, the poet cannot, without ceasing to be a poet, go beyond the word. The mystic tends toward silence, and all that is truly important in his eyes surpasses the articulated word," and even, we shall say, every affirmative mode of expression—that is why negative theology is the ultimate theology in which he finds his repose, before the Silence which is, itself, the best praise of God in the shadows of the Faith: *Silentium tibi laus.*

It must be recognized that "the most miraculous poetry approaches only remotely the regions of mystical certitude; it is also a matter of its having a different function," and therefore a different nature, a different end. "The roads are diverse by which we seek to become aware of our purest being. To those who are destined to hear its message, poetry appears clothed with a supreme dignity . . . It is the only means that we can glimpse [let us say that it is one of the two great means, the second being precisely the mystical way of union with God, with all that is involved in this way in the moral and religious order] of giving harmony to our entire being, and of creating with the same stroke harmony between our being and all that is not our being. That is what we call beauty and form, which is neither more exterior nor less really a warning and a manifestation than what we call our interior life."[11]

Let us say in conclusion that when it is a matter of mysticism and poetry, however firmly persuaded one may be of the diversity of their essences, one cannot read without emotion the beautiful texts in which all these riches are confounded and which the poets give us, they who are not charged with distinguishing . . . I think for example of that page of Lautréamont: "Poetry announces the relations that exist between the first principles and the secondary truths of life . . . Poetry discovers the laws in virtue of which theoretical politics, universal peace, are living things . . . We are far from fabricators of odes, merchants of epigrams

[11] A. Béguin, *ibid.*

against the divinity. Let us return to Confucius, to Buddha, to Socrates, to Jesus Christ, moralists who travelled the villages suffering from hunger."[12]

Everything obliges us to maintain the differences—and first of all between moralists and God; then between poetry and mysticism. But if the Poet confounds everything, would it not be because in him the formative powers of the world and of the word act together with the divine attraction toward pacification and illumination of the spirit, toward mystical knowledge and union? We must believe, since the poets tell us that they have discovered in their nocturnal navigations or divagations a Kingdom greater than the world, that an angel is pleased sometimes to tip their bark, so that they take a little "of that water" of which the Gospel speaks and do not get away without some inquietude, and some great and mysterious desire.

[12] "Preface," *Poésies,* May, 1870 (sometimes referred to as *Préface à un livre futur*).

JACQUES MARITAIN

Concerning Poetic Knowledge

THE CAREER ITSELF OF THE WORD "POETRY" SEEMS TO ME VERY instructive. It is only in relatively recent times that this word has come to designate *poetry:* previously it designated *art,* the activity of the working reason; it is in this sense that Aristotle and the ancients—and our own classical age—treated of Poetics. One might say that piercing and boring through metaphysical layers the word poetry has little by little traversed the body of the poetic work and arrived at its soul, where it has opened out into the spiritual realm. This phenomenon will not appear very surprising if one admits that poetry has only recently begun (*poets,* that is, have only recently begun) to become self-conscious in an explicit and deliberate way (and this process will never have finished).

This law of progressively becoming conscious of itself is one of the great laws of the historical development of the human being, and it is related to a property of activities of a spiritual order. The distinctive property of spirit is to be able, the ancients said, to return entirely upon itself, to accomplish a perfect reflexion, the essential thing here being not the turning back, but the grasp, the penetration of the self by the self, which is integral to it. Reflexivity is essential to the spirit, which thus grasps itself by means of itself and penetrates itself. Thence the general importance, for everything concerning culture, of the phenomenon of becoming self-conscious.

But because man is a spirit *one* in substance with the flesh, in other words, a seriously incommoded spirit, this phenomenon takes place in him slowly and with difficulty, with extraordinary delays, and it involves errors.

And it is not accomplished without unhappy accidents.

As in each case in which thought attacks a difficult task, it begins, in the conquering of new domains, and especially the interior domains of its own spiritual universe, by bringing on troubles, disasters. The human being seems to disorganize itself, and it happens in fact sometimes that these crises of growth end badly. They are nevertheless crises of growth.

Poetry in France has experienced several of them. The one in our epoch seems to me particularly significant, and never has the need to *know itself* been so violent for poetry. At these moments poetry must accomplish a double task: pursue its creative song, and turn back reflexively upon its own substance. It seems in consequence that a distinction can be made, a very summary one it is true and one which could easily become vulgar if one insisted on it too much, between two families of poets. (I shall not consider those, and they can be very great poets, who in their work carry a past moment in the life of poetry to a higher degree of perfection—which is generally the case with *great men.*)

With this reservation, then, we may say that in epochs like ours there is a family of poets who are more (I say more, I do not say exclusively) concerned with the *interior discovery of themselves* and the process of poetry's becoming self-conscious; these poets are more closely engaged in the activity and the experiments by which poetry is working on itself and renewing itself and yearns to grow in time, but precisely for this reason they are also more concerned with the typical effort of their own time. And there is another family of poets who are more concerned with continuing *poetic action* itself and that effusion of the voice of which David speaks and which goes on from age to age. Less involved in the work of historical growth of poetry, they are, in turn, freer in respect to the particular characteristics of their epoch. It is only a preponderance of aspect that I am pointing to here, and it is variable in a thousand ways; for the one family of poets like the other participates in some fashion both in the experiments and discoveries of the poetry of its time, and its work of growing, and both continue in some fashion the work of creative song.

* * *

But let us close this parenthesis. What I should like to point out is that the phenomenon of becoming self-conscious which we spoke of above is not a simple one, far from it. It occurs in a kind of labyrinthine manner, amid a host of secondary phenomena of acceleration, condensation, regression, survivance, among which genius appears from time to time to complicate things further; and it is a discontinuous phenomenon, in which successive moments may be separated by long delays.

To be sure, even among the men of the Ice Age (certain of whose designs and sculptures reveal the hand of a professional), the artist has always had a certain consciousness of his art; but in comparison with an "explicit" consciousness which is thoroughly awakened by reflexion, the "concomitant" or implicit consciousness remains a kind of sleep. And so there occurs, in the great literatures, a moment when poetry, after having created immortal works as it were in a state of sleep and not aware of itself except as a runner who at certain moments turns his head a little, begins to pass into a state of explicit self-consciousness, into a state of reflexive knowledge of that mysterious operative spiritual virtue that we call art. It is a fleeting moment, an astonishingly privileged moment. It must not be missed; it presupposes a normal and sufficiently autonomous development of civilization, a multitude of social, cultural, and spiritual conditions —and a great poet, the angels of history demand a great poet for such a moment. When one is given to them, that moment is called the moment of Aeschylus and Sophocles, the moment of Virgil, the moment of Dante. It opens the great classical epochs. After it, sometimes with it, come the grammar, the rhetoric, the recipes.

In the literatures of Christian Europe (excepting the first Italian Renaissance, and the miracle of Dante, which crowned the Middle Ages with glory at the instant when they tottered and were metamorphosed, and Petrarch is already a man of letters in the sense in which that term is understood in our day), it seems that the moment of which we have just spoken was more or less obscured by adventitious phenomena resulting from the second Renaissance. In England there was the moment of Shakespeare. In France, the moment which interests us in this connection is spread over a long period. There was, first of all, the time of Ronsard and the Pleiades, then the time of Racine, after an interval full of contrasts.

When has French poetry been richer in the invention of forms, in honest and precise ways of turning a piece of verse, than in the time of Charles of Orléans, of Marot, of Mesnard, and of Ronsard? It was the century of the rondel and the sonnet, of the ballade, of the virelay, of the rime royal; the consciousness that poetry then took of itself was the consciousness of the craftsman—a century later it was to be the consciousness of the grammarian.

For the Pleiades the injuries to poetry associated with the progress of becoming self-conscious were those deriving from archeology, and a surplus of science and verbalism which is still naive but which already causes us to miss Villon. After that, when the French spirit had felt the dangers of over-refinements in art, but reacted in the name of nature and reason, a juridical and very soon a Cartesian reason, not at all in the name of poetry, poetry experienced the greatest danger it had known in France. As a protection against the invasion of the baroque, which has produced so many masterpieces in the world, it was proclaimed: *And now let us not depart from nature by one iota!* And at the same time the consciousness of the grammarian of which I spoke a moment ago, breathing hatred against poetry, undertook, and with what ferocity, with what sureness of its mission, to sacrifice poetry to art, art having withered under this rationalist glance into artifice. It was, however, at this moment of greatest danger that poetry passed athwart grammar as a child of heaven athwart the doctors, with a supple and brilliant infallibility which was to usher in the greatest glory of that great age of prose which was our 17th century.

After Racine and La Fontaine, the fall is vertical. "Any man," writes Abbé Terrasson, "who does not think in literary matters as Descartes prescribes that one must think in matters of physics is not worthy of the present age. . . ." But in the midst of the general disaster something was acquired, and something that was not to be lost: poetry gained consciousness of itself as art, however miserable the conceptualization made of that gaining of consciousness by the disciples of Abbé Terrasson.

The question *what is art* is thenceforward a wound in its side. The classicism of the 18th century answered that question very badly, denaturing, according to the logic of clear ideas, the ancient notion of art as rectitude of the working reason, as intelligence productive of objects.

French Romanticism answered, in a manner which was primarily a movement of instinctive reaction, by rejecting together the role of the operative intellect and the absurd idea which the preceding age had formed of it. But at the same time the consciousness of art was admirably deepened. The German Romantics came in under the veil of philosophy and metaphysical enigmas, into the proper realm of poetic realities.

At the time of Gérard de Nerval and of Delacroix, then, this is what happened: by force of scrutinizing in themselves the consciousness of art, the poets ended by laying hand upon a voracious thing crouching in the depths, a thing which art does not encompass any more than the world encompasses God, and which seizes you and you no longer know where you are going. The moment arrives, in the course of the 19th century, when poetry begins to take consciousness of itself *as poetry*. Then, in a few decades, there is a series of discoveries, defeats, catastrophes, and revelations of which in my opinion one could hardly exaggerate the importance. And that was only the beginning. It required this contact of self-consciousness, of reflexive spirituality, finally to release poetry in France. I believe that what has happened to French poetry since Baudelaire has a historical importance equal in the domain of art to that of the greatest epochs of revolution and renewal of physics and astronomy in the domain of science.

I suppose that the situation of Baudelaire would be indicated precisely enough if one said that he seems to be in continuity with the best of romanticism by virtue of that deepening of the consciousness of *art* to which I just alluded, but that in reality he marks a discontinuity, a formidable mutation, because at the same instant it is *of poetry,* it is *of itself as poetry* that with him poetry becomes conscious.

The importance of this becoming conscious is immense with him, and he often insisted on it himself: "It would be prodigious that a critic should become a poet," he writes, "but it is impossible that a poet should not contain a critic." And the consciousness of poetry, it is that which constantly tortured him; the mystical knowledge of poetry, it is that which was his *abyss, moving with him;* it is that which made for the astonishing magical power of his lines (sometimes prosaic). One knows how he speaks of it many times, in particular in the first poem of *Les Fleurs du Mal*:

> Lorsque par un décret des puissances suprêmes
> Le poète apparaît en ce monde ennuyé,
> Sa mère épouvantée et pleine de blasphèmes
> Crispe ses poings vers Dieu, qui la prend en pitié . . .

or in a celebrated passage almost copied from Edgar Allan Poe, but Baudelaire had the right to consider that between himself and Poe all things were in common: "It is that immortal instinct for the beautiful which causes us to consider the earth and its spectacles as a glimpse, as a *correspondence* of heaven. The insatiable thirst for all that is beyond what life reveals is the most living proof of our immortality. It is at the same time by means of poetry and by going beyond poetry, by means of and beyond music, that the soul glimpses the splendors that lie beyond the tomb; and when an exquisite poem brings tears to the eyes, those tears are not the proof of an excess of pleasure, they are much rather the witnesses of an irritated melancholy, of an exasperated demand of the nerves, of a nature exiled in the imperfect and wishing to seize immediately, on this very earth, a revealed paradise."

It is to Baudelaire that modern poetry owes its consciousness of the quasi-theological quality, of the despotic spirituality of poetry, which for him was still called Beauty.

"The capital role of Baudelaire and of Rimbaud," we noted in the previous essay,[1] "is to have made modern art pass the frontiers of the spirit. But these are regions of supreme perils, where the hardest metaphysical problems fall upon poetry, where the battle is joined between the good angels and the bad."

I do not think Lautréamont is a good angel; he has nothing of the guardian angel about him. It is in the magic of pride that he excels; later on hate and malice will come also, or rather the spirit, the spiritual quintessence, the active extract of malice. Neither was Rimbaud a good angel, nor Baudelaire, though Baudelaire was infinitely more Christian than the other two, Christian and Jansenist and almost Manichaean. But it is all the same to poetry—poetry is no longer concerned with anything but knowing itself.

We must try to distinguish, naturally in a very schematic manner, different moments in this research with which poetry is henceforth obsessed, and which no longer asks: *what is art?* but *what is poetry?*—that poetry which is to art what grace is to the moral virtues, and which is not the peculiar privilege of poets, nor even of other artists—it can also be found in a boy who knows only how to look and to say *ah, ah, ah,* like Jeremiah, or who intoxicates himself with it to the point of frenzy or suicide without ever having said or done anything in his whole life.

* * *

One of the first aspects of poetry's taking consciousness of itself as poetry is related, it seems to me, to what is still a

[1] *Frontières de la Poésie,* 3rd ed., p. 28 (*Art & Poetry,* New York, Philosophical Library).

proper function of art, which is the creating of an object. But poetry soon transfigures this function, and this exigency: it is not an object of art that is to be created, as one might have understood the matter in the time of the Parnassians, it is a world—the poem will by itself be a self-sufficient universe, without the need of signifying anything but itself, and in which the soul must allow itself to be enclosed blindfolded, in order to receive as if through the skin, through all the surface of the body, the effluvia of night that penetrate to the heart without one's knowing how. *I am obscure like feeling,* wrote Pierre Reverdy, and his poems have the same obscurity. In order to experience their beauty, which is great, one must consent first to that obscurity. The fact is that such a preliminary consent, I mean a consent to the intentions of the artist, is always required for the understanding of a work of art and the communication which that understanding presupposes.

A second capital moment in the progressive coming to consciousness of poetry is related, I believe, to the essence of the *poetic state;* here we see poetry immersed in an infinity of infra-conscious, supra-conscious mystery to be discovered and come to know.

In a lecture delivered in Buenos Aires in the summer of 1936, Henri Michaux admirably described the disvestiture required by this frantic investigation, and by the pitiless task to which poetry thus feels itself held, to discover, to lay bare the truth of its pure substance and its own inspiration. Rhythm, rhyme, line, stanza, all the clothing of words, of music, of human intelligibility, from which the poem seems to derive its consistency, none of that is what is sought for, all of that constitutes an obstacle to the research being pursued. Are we going to reduce poetry to the impossible in order to test its resistance, and allow only an ultimate sparkling germ at the point of death to survive? Shall we not rather enter into a kind of negative theology in which the hidden essence of poetry will be attained in an incommunicable experience, from which later we shall return among men, all the means of expression now being changed and purified, I mean to say as if burned from within, by a fire which will seem to annihilate them but which will liberate unknown energies in them?

Meanwhile, insofar as it expresses that effort toward achieving consciousness which occupies us, the work itself is subjected to singular conditions of asceticism; it ceases to be a song, which it naturally demands to be, in order to become rather a revelation—secret in itself, and to which nothing remains but to try to touch our hearts in forbidden ways—of the secret functioning of the poetic powers in the substance of the poet.

To do away with words, with all the load of falsehood and the more-or-less, of parasitical associative connotations which they involve, to do away with words, or create new words, or transsubstantiate the old ones, is to leave off the ordinary play of ideas and concepts as well as the rational, social, and human life; it is to enter a savage world where there is no longer anything to protect us, and, finally, it is to take leave, in a way, of the human race—*aber ich will kein Mensch sein,* but I do not want to be a man . . .

There is the great night, the night which stirs, and the desire to lose one's being.

We have just spoken of a second aspect or moment in the coming to consciousness of poetry *as poetry,* and which concerns above all the poetic state. I think that one could, at least by abstraction, discern a third, deeper still than the other two, and which would be related rather to *poetic knowl-*

edge, I mean to the knowledge of reality, and of the interior of things, or their reverse side, proper to poetry or to the spirit of poetry.

The more deeply poetry becomes conscious of itself, the more deeply it becomes conscious of its power of *knowing,* and of the mysterious movement by which, as Jules Supervielle put it one day, it approaches the sources of being.

Here we arrive at the crucial point of the debate, and at particularly difficult philosophical questions, but questions which it would be a lack of courage not to want to consider. Before treating them rapidly I should like to remark that the three moments of which I have spoken are related to diverse modalities of the coming to consciousness of poetry, not to diverse chronological instants; they can take place at the same time; and, for example, it is to the ultimate moment, to the moment of *poetic knowledge,* that Rimbaud is carried at the very start, thus entering at once the burning core of the flame.

II

When a philosopher reflects on poetry, he perceives first of all, as we noted above, that poetry is situated in the line of art or creative activity. Now the end of art as such is not to know, but to produce or *create*—not in the mode of nature, as radium produces helium or as a living being engenders another, but in the way of spirit and of liberty; here it is a matter of the productivity of the intellect *ad extra.*[2]

[2] There are some *speculative* arts, like logic. As such, they remain purely intellectual, and the will has nothing to do with them, unless with the exercising of them. This is a limiting case in which the notion of art is retained, and even carried to an extreme of purity, because there is a *factibile* here, but one which remains purely intellectual and interior to the spirit. Note that one can speak of the poetry of logic as of that of mathematics, insofar as logic is an object that one contemplates; but at the heart of logic itself poetry and poetic knowledge have no place. If logic is an example of the purest art, it is seen how poetry in its pure state, which will be treated below, and art in its pure state can find themselves in diametrical opposition.

The activity of the intelligence in itself is a kind of manifestation: it produces *within* itself its mental words, which are, for it, its means of knowing, but which are also effects of its spiritual *abundance*, internal expressions or manifestations of what it knows.

And by a natural *superabundance* it tends of itself to express and manifest outside itself, to sing: it abounds not only in its own word, it demands to superabound in a work, a natural desire which, because it will go beyond the frontiers of the intelligence itself, cannot be realized without the movement to which it entices the will and the appetitive powers. These then cause the intellect to go out from itself, in accord with its natural wish, and thus determine its original impulse of movement, and, in an altogether general way, the *poeticity* (in the Aristotelian sense of the word) or the operative practicity of the intellect. After this original determination, the activity of art will develop in a line which is much more purely intellectual—and in which the human will with its own ends will be much less involved—than the line of moral activity (ethical practicity).

Thus we understand that in general, in all practicity of the spirit, the will or appetite has a certain part, a variable one moreover, and that, in the special case of the practicity which issues in the making of objects, that part is less than in the case of ethical practicity, since the "idea" of the work-to-be-made is already a practical idea in and by itself (because in itself it presupposes that primitive movement of the intellect toward some being to be produced, in which the will intervened).

Such is, we believe, reduced to its pure and essential metaphysical exigencies, the primary root of the poetic activity in the sense of *activity of art*. This metaphysical root can be obscured by an immense empirical, psychological, and sociological conditioning, and by the more apparent ends of utility, whether they be for example the magical ends of the most primitive painters or the need of tools which is connatural to man; this metapyhsical root is presupposed by these ends and by this conditioning.

Understood thus, the activity of art is not related in itself to a need of communicating *to others* (this need is real and in fact intervenes inevitably in artistic activity, but it does not *define* it); it is related essentially to the need of speaking and manifesting in a work-to-be-made—by virtue of spiritual superabundance and even though there were no one to see or hear (which would in other ways be a cruel anomaly). This is so true that it happens sometimes that the artist suffers more profoundly from that very public with which he wishes to enter into communion when he is "understood" by it than when he is "misunderstood": to be understood diminishes him, puts him out of his element; he wonders if his work does not lack some deeper quality which, if it were there, would not have been communicable. It is not for man that he produces his work, or at least it is for future generations which he conceives of as in some way immaterial because they do not exist. What he wants is not to be understood, it is to endure in history.

What follows from all this, from the point of view of knowledge?

The activity of art is not in itself an activity of knowledge, but of creation; what it aims at is to *make an object* according to the internal exigencies and the proper good of that object.

It presupposes, it is true, it utilizes a *previous* knowledge: being an intellectual or spiritual productivity, it cannot in fact be content with the object itself, toward which it tends as a simply productive activity, an object which is enclosed in a genus. As *intellectual* activity it tends in a certain fashion, even in its act of creating, toward being, which transcends all genera. It will be necessary then that this object which it forms, whether a vase of clay or a fishing boat, be *significant* of something else than itself, be a sign at the same time as an object; it will be necessary that some sense animate it and make it say more than it is. From which it follows that art, while it is productive in its essence, always supposes a moment of contemplation, and the work of art a melody, that is to say, a sense animating a form.[3] It is upon this fact that Aristotle based his declaration that imitation is inherent to art; and this, as the word imitation clearly indicates, relates primarily and on the most apparent visible level (but not the most profound[4]) to a (speculative) knowledge previous to the activity of art and *pre-supposed* by it, but extrinsic to it; to knowledge, to all the ordinary human knowledge which the artist procures for himself in opening his eyes and his intelligence upon the things of the world and upon culture. The activity of art begins *after* that, because it is a creative activity and because, in itself, it does not ask that the mind *be formed* by an object to be known, but that it *form* an object to proffer into being.

* * *

With these considerations, however, we have reached only the exterior of the mystery. Let us try to go further.

What is it that an act of thought which in its essence is creative, which forms something in the realm of being instead of being formed by things, expresses and manifests in producing its work, if not the very being and substance of

[3] Cf. Arthur Lourié, *De la Mélodie, "La Vie Intellectuelle,"* 25 December, 1936.

[4] On the profoundest, most hidden level, it is to poetic knowledge itself that the Aristotelian notion of imitation must be related. Cf. below, pp. 61-62 and p. 103, note 1.

him who creates? But the substance of a man is obscure to himself; it is in receiving and suffering things, in awaking to the world, that it awakes to itself. The poet, we have said elsewhere, cannot express his own substance in a work except on the condition that things resound in him, and that within him, in a single awakening, those things and his own substance rise together out of sleep. It is thus as if all that he discerns and divines in things he discerns and divines as inseparable from himself and his emotion, indeed as himself, and so he grasps obscurely his own being, with a knowledge which will only come to fruition in being creative.[5] That is why he shows the Grail to others and does not see it himself.[6] His intuition, the creative intuition or emotion, is an obscure grasping of the self and things together in a knowledge by union or by connaturality which is not completed, does not fructify, does not achieve its word, except in the work and which with all its vital energy moves toward making and producing. Here is a knowledge that is different enough from what we commonly call knowledge, a knowledge which is not expressible in ideas and in judgments, but which is rather experience than knowledge, and creative experience, for it wants to be expressed, and is expressible only in a work. This knowledge is neither previous to nor presupposed by the creative activity, but inviscerated in it, consubstantial with the movement toward the work, and this is, properly speaking, what I call *poetic knowledge,* understanding that the word knowledge is an analogical term, which designates here a knowledge in which the mind does not tend, as toward its repose, toward "having become the things" it knows, but toward "having produced a thing in being." *Poetic knowledge* is thus the secret, vital virtue of that

[5] Cf. *Frontières de la Poésie,* p. 197.
[6] Jean Cocteau, *Les Chevaliers de la Table Ronde.*

spiritual germ that the ancients called the idea of the work, the working idea, or the idea of the artisan.

It has become conscious of itself at the same time as poetry has; or rather, that divining plunge *is* poetry itself, it is the spirit which, in the sensible and through the sensible, in passion and through passion, in and through the density of experience, seizes the secret *meaning* of things and of itself in order to embody them in matter; the same meaning constituting at the same time the meaning thus perceived in being and the meaning which animates the work produced, or what I called a moment ago the melody of every authentic work of art, so that in this meaning or melody the work and the depth of existence and of the poet, the signifying and the signified, communicate, exist as two in a single song and in a single intentionality.

Ancient and modern philosophers have speculated a great deal about poetry; but, necessarily, from without. We admit —I tried to say why a moment ago—that it is in the 19th century, with the preparations made by the romantics, and above all with Baudelaire and Rimbaud, that poetry began *among the poets* to become deliberately and systematically conscious of itself. Every new consciousness is accompanied by a risk of perversion. The risk here was that poetry would want to escape from the line of the work-to-be-made in order to turn back upon the soul itself, thinking to fill the soul with pure knowledge and become its absolute.

Now it is quite true that one may be a poet without producing—without having yet produced—any work of art, but if one is a poet one is virtually turned towards operation. It is of the essence of poetry to be in the operative line, as a tree is in the line of producing fruit. But in becoming conscious of itself, poetry in some measure frees itself from the work-to-be-made, in the measure in which to know oneself is to turn back upon oneself.

At the same time poetry disengages its active principle in a pure state, I mean poetic knowledge itself, that indescribable and fecund experience which Plato called enthusiasm, and which the brief indications given above tried to characterize. And at that instant there awakens in poetry a desire hidden in its transcendental character and in its very spirituality, a metaphysical aspiration, to pass beyond, to transgress the limits which enclose it in a nature, at a certain degree on the scale of beings. At once poetry enters into conflict with art, with that art in whose way its nature condemns it to go: when art demands to form intellectively, according to a creative idea, poetry demands to suffer, to listen, to descend to the roots of being, to an unknown that no idea can circumscribe. "For *I* is an other," said Rimbaud,[7] and could one better define that engulfment in the *inhabited* subject which is poetic knowledge? An instant of vertigo is enough then. If poetry loses its footing, there it is, detached from its operative ends. It becomes a means of knowing; it no longer wants to create, but to know. When art demands to make, poetry, loosed from its natural ties, demands to know.

But knowledge—what a temptation, what an absolute! And such a knowledge, which engages the whole of man! And which gives the world to man in causing him to suffer the world! If, freed (or believing itself freed) from the relativities of art, poetry finds a soul which nothing else occupies, nothing confronting it, it is going to develop an appalling appetite to know, which will vampirise all that is metaphysical in man, and all that is carnal as well.

[7] Letter to Paul Demeny ("Lettre du Voyant"), 15 May, 1871, first published by Paterne Berrichon in *La Nouvelle Revue Française,* October, 1912.

The experience of Rimbaud is decisive here. Whereas later, while appealing to Rimbaud, the surrealists were to try to use poetry as an instrument for their quasi-"scientific" curiosity, Rimbaud himself obeyed, he consciously and voluntarily obeyed the ultimate tyrannical exigencies of poetic knowledge let loose in its full state of savagery—it is that which made him search for all the treasures of the spirit in the forbidden byways of a heroic and "debauched" banditry.

A moment ago I quoted from the *Lettre du Voyant,* in which, precisely, while explaining that he is giving himself to knowledge, he declares in the same breath that he is "debauching" himself.[8] Let us limit ourselves to this capital text, and to the evidence it offers us, the significance of which one's commentary would never exhaust.

"The first study of a man who wants to be a poet"—who *wants* to be a poet, says Rimbaud: taking consciousness, a deliberate undertaking, and there already the trap is hidden —"is knowledge of himself, complete. He seeks his soul, he inspects it, he tries it, learns it. As soon as he knows it, he must cultivate it: that seems simple: in every brain a natural development is accomplished; so many *egotists* proclaim themselves authors; there are many more of them who attribute to themselves their intellectual progress! But it is a matter of making the soul monstrous: in the manner of the comprachicos, what! Imagine a man planting and cultivating warts on his face. I say it is necessary to *be a seer,* to make oneself a *seer.*

"The poet makes himself a *seer* by a long, immense, and reasoned *derangement* of *all the senses.* All the forms of love, of suffering, of madness; he searches in himself, he drains from himself all the poisons, that he may keep only their quintessences. Ineffable torture, in which he needs all the faith, all the superhuman force, in which he becomes among

[8] Cf. Benjamin Fondane, *Rimbaud le Voyou.*

all the critical case, the great criminal, the great outcast—and the supreme Savant!— For he arrives at the *unknown*—since he cultivates his soul, already richer than any! He arrives at the *unknown;* and when, frantic, he would finish by losing the understanding of his visions, he has seen them! Let him croak in the bouncing about by unheard-of and unnameable things; there will come other horrible laborers: they will begin at the horizons where the other gave way!"[9]

The conclusion, enunciated with an astonishing lucidity in *A Season in Hell,* was inevitable. Poetry aiming, in order to realize itself in full plenitude, to deliver itself from every condition of existence, poetic knowledge exalting itself to the point of claiming *absolute* life, engages itself in a dialectic which kills it. It wants to be everything and give everything, the act, sanctity, transsubstantiation, the miracle; it has charge of humanity. And whatever it does, it is limited by nature, in reality, to one line only, a particular and very humble one indeed, to the line of art and of the work-to-be-made. In the end there is nothing left but to lapse into silence, to renounce the work and poetry at the same time. Rimbaud not only stopped writing, he avenged himself on poetry, applied himself to casting it from him as a monster.

* * *

The preceding considerations suggest to us the idea that poetry does not *of itself* accord with anything other than itself, not with faith, nor with metaphysics, nor with sanctity: just as in general nothing which reaches toward the infinite accords of itself with anything else. It is folly, as we have just seen, to want it *alone* in the soul, But *with the rest*—with all the other virtues and energies of the spirit, how should it get along? The fact is that all these energies, insofar as

[9] Letter to Paul Demeny ("Lettre du Voyant"), cited above.

they pertain to the transcendental universe, aspire like poetry to surpass their nature and to infinitise themselves. They compose the one for the other a condition of existence, they help one another exist, but all the while hating one another (in a sense, for they love one another too), imposing limits on one another, seeking to reduce one another to impotence. It is only in this conflict that they can exist and grow. Art, poetry, metaphysics, prayer, contemplation, each one is wounded, struck traitorously in the best of itself, and that is the very condition of its living. *Man* unites them by force, weeping all his tears, dying every day, and thus he wins his peace and their peace.

III

The experience of Rimbaud was too complete and too hard for the lesson to be learned from it. In spite of Rimbaud, in spite of *A Season in Hell,* still attempting to enter by main force further into the consciousness of poetry, still persisting in this travail, and, what is more, making a glory of it, poets had to commit the same error of misdirection. But this time pretending to continue the trip up this blind alley, to go to the end of the world and beyond the world in a motionless vehicle: and can this not be accomplished by way of illusion, and thanks to a certain magic?

It is in its attempt to use poetry to fulfill the desires of man and his thirst for knowledge, and his need to see the face of the absolute, that surrealism has for us an exceptional historical interest.

According to the remark of M. Marcel Raymond cited above, "to attest that the game is not yet up, that all can perhaps be saved—that was the essential of the surrealist message." In short, the surrealists also have been victims of poetic knowledge. In the beginning for them, it was a matter above all of rediscovering, as Raïssa Maritain writes in the first of the essays here collected, "that river of the spirit which flows under all our customary activity, that profound, authentic reality, foreign to all formulae, perceived in those 'minutes of abandonment to hidden forces' which vivify."[10] The fact was, I doubt not, that they had actually known those privileged instants of natural ecstasy in which the soul "reimmerses itself so to speak in its source, and from which it issues renewed and fortified" by the poetic experience. That experience they had, let that fortune not be denied them! It is what makes for the value and the tragedy of their adventure. They had it while turning away, by reflection, from the poetic work and from song, to engage themselves desperately in the circumvolutions of the consciousness. But they were caught in the trap. Wresting poetry almost completely from its natural finalities, they wanted to make of it a means of speculative knowledge, an instrument of science, a method of metaphysical discovery.

And they not only confounded poetry with metaphysics; they confounded it with morality, and they confounded it with sanctity. They charged it thus with a burden it could not bear. What end, then, could its power of seduction serve, if not to astonish us with tricks, to open up to us a world of mere appearances and of tinsel?

Finally, because they confounded the passivity of the poetic experience with that of psychic automatism, the surrealists believed that the means par excellence, or rather the unique source, of poetry was the delivering of images, the liberating of charges of emotion and dream accumulated in our animal sub-conscious filled with desires and signs. What then developed among the poets of that generation was a remarkable sharpness of instinct to confuse the traces and to disconcert the mind by means of surprise and the stimulative wounding of the imagination; and of how much more value is this

[10] Raïssa Maritain, "Sense and Non-Sense in Poetry," p. 11, above.

allusive rapidity than the classic *discursus!* But in itself, if one remains at that point, it is only another technique, a feat of taste and of talent.

From all this, and from the history and the disappointment of the surrealist attempt, I conclude that errors can occur in the coming to consciousness of poetry, as in every human achievement of consciousness; that is one of the inevitable dangers, as we noted at the beginning of this essay, that the life and progress of the spirit carries with it in man.

To imagine, however, that coming to consciousness in itself, or progress in reflexivity, is a bad thing, a thing which by its nature tends to deform, would be to fall into a sort of Manichaean pessimism, which is, moreover, as false as possible, if it is true that reflexivity is, as I have said, a typical property of the spirit. In the very errors of coming to consciousness there are always coexistent discoveries.

Not to know what one is doing—it is thus, especially when it is a matter of self-forgetfulness due to a superior motion, that one makes the most beautiful things and performs the most generous acts. But not to know what one is doing—it is thus also that one commits the greatest crimes (and has the best chance also of being pardoned for them). All in all, other things being equal, it is better, however dangerous it be, and to whatever sanctions one expose oneself, to *know what one is doing*.

In any case, for that matter, we do not have the choice. When the naïve ages are past, they are *quite* past. The only resource left to us is a better and purer self-consciousness.

* * *

May I point out here the danger, which does not seem to me totally imaginary, of another possible error in the opposite direction? Among the normal reactions which take place against the experiences of these last years, it could happen—if we had to do with a simple phenomenon, as if of a pendulum, of action and reaction—that after having wished to give all to the subterranean powers of the world of images, one would turn, again in too *exclusive* a manner, and as if they alone counted, toward the powers, sometimes not less obscure, and the fecundity proper to the world of intelligence and discourse. And God preserve me from speaking ill of the intelligence! But it must not be mediocre, and in poetry it is far from being everything: error, said Pascal, comes from exclusion—that is the point I wish to make.

I add that in fact, when one invokes the primacy of the intelligence, not in order to seek out the internal hierarchies of the soul but in order to give passwords and collective instructions, it is not the intelligence as seeker of wisdom, the true intelligence (which is rarely met with), that profits from the operation; it is the facile and social intelligence, anti-metaphysical, empirical, and rationalizing, and which is found everywhere. And for this latter kind of intelligence poetry can very well on occasion express philosophical ideas, and sing *de natura rerum*—the foundation of the authority of such intelligence is neither metaphysical nor mystical, but only psychological, or even sociological.

If then things should take the course I have just indicated, by way of a simple reaction on the surface, we should run the risk of forgetting that though poetry cannot be confounded with metaphysics, it yet responds to a metaphysical need of the spirit of man, and is metaphysically justified. And though it cannot be confounded with sanctity, nor charged with the duties of sanctity, yet in its own line, which is not that of the good of man but rather of the good of the work, it involves a *kind* of sanctity, demands purifications and woes which are in a certain way symbolic of those of souls on the way toward the perfection of love. And we should run the risk of forgetting that the source of poetry is not the intelligence alone, from whatever depths it may surge up in certain men.

In brief, it could happen, on the pretext of latinity, and of the primacy of the reason (of a reason more or less rationalist), and in the name, if one may speak thus, of a Mediterranean catholicity, that a neo-classical reaction would ask poetry to *exhibit ideas and sentiments,* to charge itself with the rubbish of human notions in their verbosity and their natural meanness, and to fabricate *versified discourses* for the delectation of the formal intelligence. We should then see born a poetics "of abundance," of verbal abundance and of intellectual reduplication. And the word would again become master, the glory of the word, the endless and buzzing heroism of language—and all the stupidity of man.

Poetry is ontology, certainly, and even, according to the great saying of Boccaccio, poetry is theology. But in the sense that it finds its birth in the soul in the mysterious sources of being, and reveals them in some way by its own creative movement. Though the unconscious from which it proceeds is not, unless secondarily, the Freudian unconscious of instincts and images, it is, however, an unconscious more vital and deeper, the unconscious of the spirit *at its source*—hidden from the reasoning intelligence in that density of the soul where all the soul's powers have their common origin.

In short, it is toward the totality of his being that the poet is led back, if he is docile to the gift he has received, and consents to enter into the depths and let himself be laid bare. We think that this poetics of integrality, or rather of integration, not by an effort of voluntary concentration, but by the quietude of creative retreat and of poetic knowledge left to its own nature, is that which the present situation of poetry allows us to hope for—because it answers to the best and purest achievement of self-consciousness that one can expect from poetry today.

Let us transcribe here the witness of the poet who composed the first part of this book: "Born in a vital experience, life itself, poetry asks to be expressed by life-bearing signs, signs which conduct the one who receives them back to the ineffability of the original experience. Since in this contact all the sources of our faculties have been touched, the echo of it ought itself to be total . . ." "Song, poetry in all its forms, seeks to liberate a substantial experience . . . The brooding repose which is provided by such an experience acts as a refreshing bath, a rejuvenation and purification of the spirit . . . We cannot esteem too highly the profundity of the quiet which all our faculties then enjoy. It is a concentration of all the energies of the soul, but a peaceful, tranquil concentration, which involves no tension; the soul enters into its repose, in this place of refreshment and of peace superior to any feeling. It dies . . . but only to revive in exaltation and enthusiasm, in that state which is wrongly called 'inspiration,' because inspiration was nothing other, indeed, than this very repose itself, in which it escaped from sight. Now the mind, reinvigorated and enlivened, enters into a happy activity, so easy that everything seems to be given to it at once and, as it were, from outside. In reality, everything was there, in the shadow, hidden in the spirit and in the blood; everything that is going to be manifested in operation was there, but we knew it not. We knew neither how to discover it nor how to make use of it before having re-immersed ourselves in those tranquil depths."[11]

[11] *Ibid.*, pp. [9;] [26], above.

It is in no sense a matter of diminishing the role of the intelligence, nor the importance of intelligibility, of human experience, of conscious metaphysics involved in the poetic work, especially when that work is a tragedy for example, or a drama or epic. I say only that the fire of creative intuition must be hot enough to consume these materials, and not to be extinguished by them. Discursive lucidity is itself an integral part of the poetry of a Shakespeare, but the lucidity and all the logic, all the rationality and all the acquired knowledge, have been brought back to the secret source of refreshment and of peace of which we spoke a moment ago, in order to be transfigured and vivified there, and brought, if I may so express it, to the *creative state,* because they have all become poetic knowledge there. In that interior source the words of the tribe and the human notions lose that verbosity and that natural meanness which we referred to a few moments ago, because they undergo there, if I may so express it, a second birth.

Then, then alone, the poet has neither to escape from language nor submit himself to it, because the language is newly born in him and of him, as on the first morning of the terrestrial paradise.

All of these considerations suggest to us the conclusion that "in order that the life of the creative spirit grow without ceasing, conformably to its law, it is necessary that it deepen without ceasing the center of subjectivity where, in suffering the things of the world and those of the soul, it awakens to itself . . . Creation takes place at different levels in the substance of the soul—thereby each person shows what he is—and the more the poet grows, the more the level of the creative intuition descends into the density of his soul."[12] The more the poet at the same time simplifies himself, so much the more he rejects masks, consents to say what he is, feels the worth of human communion. The whole question for him is to have—along with a strong enough art (which can be learned)—a deep enough soul, which cannot be learned. Woe itself is not sufficient.

In an important study on melody, Arthur Lourié wrote a few years ago: "Modern music has lost the melodic element to the same degree that poetry has lost the lyric element." And what Lourié called melody here is an element of an order quite apart, which is developed in time but is not of time, and which is born of a breaking of the connections of time. "Melody, by itself," he writes further, "is not connected with any action, and does not lead to any action. It is like an end in itself. The *motif* serves to justify the action; the *theme* is a means of developing a thought. The *melody*, itself, serves no end. It gives liberation."[13] That is to say that the melody is the very spirit of the music and the revelation of the intimate being of the musician. There is in poetry an element of the same nature, which is the spirit of poetry, and that revelation in act of the intimate person of the poet which is the same thing as poetic knowledge. I do not believe it to be true that modern poetry has lost that element. It has dissimulated it more or less, has been ashamed to avow it too loudly. But it is that element above all that it is trying to grasp in becoming conscious of itself.

There is at this moment in France a singular increase in poetry. I know some young poets who inspire me with a great confidence. I believe that their task will be to liberate the element of which we are speaking, that spring of living

[12] *Frontières de la Poésie,* pp. 199-200.
[13] Arthur Lourié, *op. cit.*

water born in the spiritual depths of the person, revealing, like melody, "the undisfigured essence of what is," and not "the lie imagined by its author."

The condition imposed—and it is dangerous enough to wound or to kill the seekers—is that the waters of that source be *true* enough, and well up from sufficient depth, to be able to carry away and transfigure the astonishing vegetation of images whose secret rites poetry has been learning for twenty years, but which by themselves are still only matter. If modern poetry must become more ontological, get into closer contact with being, with human and terrestrial reality (and perhaps also with divine reality), it is not by cares foreign to its nature and a well-intentioned zeal that it will accomplish this, but only through that lyric element which is almost as hidden as grace, hidden in the deepest of creative sources.

THREE PHILOSOPHICAL CONCLUSIONS

After this metaphysical description, we should like to propose briefly three more systematic conclusions.

In the first place: poetic knowledge is a knowledge *by affective connaturality* of the *operative* type, or tending to express itself in a work. It is not a knowledge "by mode of knowledge," it is a knowledge by mode of instinct or inclination, by mode of resonance in the subject, and which proceeds toward creating a work.

In such a knowledge it is the created object, the *work made,* the poem, the picture, the symphony, which plays the role of the mental word and of the *judgment* in speculative knowledge.[14]

It follows from this that poetic knowledge is not fully

[14] To eliminate all confusion, let it be noted that it is of *poetic knowledge* precisely understood, not of the *artistic habitus* that we are speaking here. The habitus of art produces its fruit in the practical *judgment* on the work to be made; poetic knowledge, in the *work done.*

conscious except in the work made; it does not completely attain consciousness except in the work—in the work which in other ways materializes it and disperses it in some way in order to bring it back into a new unity, that of the thing posed in being.

Precisely as knowledge or experience (and more experience than knowledge), and taken separately from the production of the work, poetic knowledge is, in its essential character, unconscious—barely signalled to the consciousness by a shock which is at the same time emotional and intellectual, or by a spurt of song, which gives notice of its presence but does not at all express it.

We are here confronted by an unconscious of a special type. As we noted above, it is the unconscious of the spirit *at its source,* quite a different thing from the Freudian unconscious of images and instincts.

If on the other hand, it is remarked that the idea as such (insofar as it is distinguished from the judgment) is not necessarily conscious, one understands that it is with good reason that the ancients designated the intentional form of poetic knowledge not as a judgment but as an *idea,* as a factive or formative idea—which, inasmuch as it is nourished by poetic knowledge and vivified by the grace of poetry, is at the same time intuition and emotion.[15]

Our second conclusion concerns the relation of poetic knowledge to other kinds of knowledge by connaturality.

Leaving aside the knowledge by tendential or affective connaturality with the ends of human action, which is at the

[15] If in their theory of the artistic idea the old schoolmen seem to have neglected this character—essential to the human creative intuition—of enveloping a knowledge by emotion and by affective connaturality, it is that they considered art and the creative activity above all as theologians, and concerned themselves with the analogical values according to which the activity of art is proper to God as well as to the human creature.

heart of *prudential* knowledge, we will distinguish three other kinds of knowledge by connaturality:

(1) A knowledge by intellectual connaturality with reality as *conceptualisable* and rendered proportionate in act to the human intellect. It goes along with the development of the *habitus* of the intelligence; and it is from this knowledge that comes the *intuition*—intellectual and expressible in a mental work—of the philosopher, the scientist, of him who knows by mode of knowledge.

(2) A knowledge by either intellectual or affective connaturality with reality as *non-conceptualisable* and at the same time *contemplated,* in other words as non-objectifiable in notions and yet as a terminus of objective union. This is the knowledge of *contemplation:* whether it is a matter of a natural contemplation attaining, if that be possible, a transcendant reality inexpressible in itself in a human mental word, by means of a supra- or para-conceptual intellection; or of a supernatural contemplation attaining as object the divine reality inexpressible in itself in any created word, by means of the union of love (*amor transit in conditionem objecti*) and by a resonance in the subject, becomes a means of knowing.

(3) A knowledge by *affective* connaturality with reality as *non-conceptualisable* because *awakening to themselves the creative depths of the subject*—I mean by connaturality with reality according as reality comes to be buried in subjectivity itself in its quality of intellectually productive existence, and according as it is attained in its concrete and existential consonance with the subject *as subject.* This is *poetic* knowledge: radically factive or operative, since, being inseparable from the productivity of the spirit (owing to the fact that the connaturality which awakens it actuates the subject as subject, or as center of productive vitality and spiritual emana-

tion), and being unable nevertheless to issue in a concept *ad intra,* it can only issue in a work *ad extra.*[16]

It seems likely that in the case of all those who have great intuitive gifts there is an element of poetic knowledge, in the sense that it underlies philosophic and scientific intuition and works together with it, and that by a kind of inevitable psychological resonance it also accompanies, be it only virtually, the natural and supernatural contemplation of which it is an analogue. But it is essentially distinct from the one and the other.

Being a knowledge by affective connaturality, the knowledge of supernatural contemplation itself awakens in the soul the poetic instinct, though it be in an entirely rudimentary and virtual manner. That is why it is natural to the mystical experience to be expressed lyrically. But insofar as it is expressed, and wells up in song, it is that the mystical experience itself—when the contemplative is also a poet—has provoked in the depths of the subjectivity a present poetic knowledge of the realities mystically experienced; or it may be also that by virtue of the superabundance of a perfect actuation it pours out gratuitously, without the least operative tension, in words which can be richer in poetry than the work of a poet, and which all the same, in the case in question, come not from a poetic knowledge, but from the excess of a higher experience.

[16] The distinction of these two different modes (nos. 2 and 3) of transcending conceptualisation can be regarded as a free gloss of the following texts of Saint Thomas. "*Poetica scientia* est de his quae propter defectum veritatis non possunt a ratione capi; unde oportet quod quasi quibusdam similitudinibus ratio seducatur; *theologia* autem est de his quae sunt supra rationem; et ideo modus symbolicus utrique communis est, cum neutra rationi proportionetur." (I *Sent.* prol., q. 1, a. 5, ad 3.) "Sicut poetica non capiuntur in ratione humana, propter defectum veritatis quae est in eis; ita etiam ratio humana perfecte capere non potest divina, propter excedentem ipsorum veritatem. Ed ideo utrobique opus est repraesentatione per sensibiles figuras." (*Sum. Theol.,* I-II, 101, 2, ad 2.)

It is also to be remarked that poetic knowledge, like the knowledge of contemplation (when it expresses itself), employs similitudes and symbols—in order to *seduce the reason,* as St. Thomas says;[17] precisely because both of these kinds of knowledge have to do, in different ways, with the non-conceptualisable.

But what we should like above all to remember is that being in itself radically operative, oriented toward the creation of a work, poetic knowledge does not liberate itself *in the mode of knowledge* except in turning back upon itself in a reflexive consciousness in which it is detached in a way (in a purely virtual way when everything remains normal) from its natural finalities. It does not reveal itself thus to itself as knowledge and as appetite for knowledge without running the risk in some measure of "perversion," or misdirection, of which we have spoken. And if this misdirection occurs, if this separation from its natural ends takes place really and effectively, poetic knowledge engenders an endless voracity to know—endless because resulting from turning aside from the natural ends.

And being unable to end either in a *work* (which it renounces and from which it turns away), or in a *speculative conceptualisation* (which is repugnant to it and for which it has not the means), it involves the spirit in a tragedy, strangely instructive and fecund in discoveries, but, in itself, monstrous.

In short, poetry *is* knowledge, incomparably: knowledge-experience and knowledge-emotion, existential knowledge, knowledge which is the germ of a work (and which does not know itself, and which is not *for* knowing). To make of it a *means of knowledge,* an instrument of knowledge, to take it out of its proper mode of being in order to procure that

[17] See I *Sent.,* prol., q. 1, a. 5, ad 3 (text cited in the previous note); and *In Johan.,* cap. 7, lect. 2.

which it is, is to pervert it. In this sense it is a sin for the poet to eat of the fruit of the tree of knowledge. Let us add concerning the poets who have suffered most from this evil that their work, insofar as they have created works, is a victory over it, and all the more precious.

The third and last conclusion concerns the law of *transgression* of which we spoke a moment ago, and according to which all energies of a transcendental order aspire, inefficaciously, to go beyond the nature enclosed in a genus which they have in man, in order to follow the inclination of their transcendentality, and ultimately, tend toward pure act and infinitisation.

Taken as transcendental and in its analogical polyvalence, a perfection of the transcendental order is not an essence, a specific nature; it is found in an essentially varied manner in a series of distinct specific essences. If here or there it follows the aspiration of its transcendentality taken as such, it aspires to go beyond these natures, it aspires in an inefficacious manner to pass beyond, to become in a certain way what it is in the pure Act.[18]

An energy of transcendental order like that of metaphysics aspires in this way to the vision of God; an energy like that of mystical contemplation aspires to the divine liberty. It is only at the moment of becoming conscious of itself, when

[18] St. Thomas (*Sum. Theol.*, I, 63, 3) explains that a thing constituted with a given nature (with a given nature enclosed in a species and a genus) cannot aspire to a superior specific nature, "sicut asinus non appetit esse equus: quia, si transferretur in gradum superioris naturae, jam ipsum non esset." But precisely the perfections of the transcendental order, not being enclosed in a species and a genus, do not lose their being when they pass from what they are in an inferior species to what they are in a superior species; on the contrary, they approach their "maximum" of being. That is why it is possible that in a given nature an energy of the transcendental order aspires in an inefficacious manner to pass in some way into what it is in a superior nature, and especially in the *Ipsum esse subsistens.*

it discovers itself reflexively, that poetry also discovers such an aspiration within itself. This may tend toward pure creation (to create as God creates, that is the torment of certain great artists, who in the end, by force of wishing to be purely creators, and to owe nothing to the vision of the beings which God has had the indiscretion to make in front of them, have no other resource than that of artistically forcing and ravaging their art); or, on the contrary, if poetry detaches itself from its operative ends in the way we indicated a moment ago, if in becoming conscious of itself it takes a wrong direction, this aspiration will tend toward a kind of divine intuition or divine experience of the world and the soul, known as God knows them, from within, and within the essence of their Poet. And this will be the more violent in proportion as the poetic experience has been truly and really detached from its natural finalities.

JACQUES MARITAIN

The Experience of the Poet

M. MARCEL DE CORTE HAS PUBLISHED IN VARIOUS REVIEWS, IN particular the *Revue Thomiste,*[1] some studies in aesthetics whose importance is in our eyes considerable. Handling with a singular doctrinal force, and a remarkable metaphysical attention to the evidence of the poets, the means of discovery furnished by Thomism, he brings profound insights to bear upon the ontology of poetry, insights which will aid seekers bent on dangerous explorations to find their way into one of the most secret domains of philosophy.

The convergence of his research with that reported in this little book appears significant to us. We see in it a far from negligible indication of the objective value of the results to which, on the one side and on the other, we have been led; and it is no small thing that in matters as obscure as these it is shown to be possible to work in agreement and to advance in common, when so often philosophers suffer from having to employ incommunicable lexicons. The divergences which exist under these conditions have only the more chance of designating especially delicate difficulties, the treatment of

[1] *Revue Thomiste,* Nov.-Dec. 1937, Jan. 1938 (Ontologie de la Poésie). See also *Hermès,* June 1936, and *Revue de Philosophie,* May-June, 1936.

which promises to be particularly fecund. The remarks which follow attempt to render precise some of these difficulties.[2]

I. *Poetic experience and creation.* In itself the poetic experience is in the line of making or of creation; normally poetic knowledge is ordered not toward knowing but toward producing. Why is this so? Why is the object of the poetic experience (but this word "object," just in itself, risks introducing verbal confusions into the discussion—let us rather say the *percept* of the poetic experience or *that which is apprehended*), why is the percept of the poetic experience non-conceptualisable as such, why is it, as distinguished from the percept of contemplation, not ordered *to knowing* but *to being expressed in a work,* to being cast into being? Why is it rather a source of creative activity than a termination in objective union?

In order to answer this question it would be necessary to turn one's attention first toward *subjectivity* as such. Subjectivity truly and properly so called begins only with personality, or rather the two are aspects of the same thing. Subjectivity is intimately connected with the privileges of spirituality and of immanence proper to the personality itself. A subjectivity is a spiritual subsistence and existence, which are radically active, sources of the superexistence of knowledge and the superexistence of love; and if in the case of these activities all specification comes from the object, all the vitality, on the other hand, and all the vital productivity come from the subjectivity itself. A subjectivity appears thus, by virtue of its most deeply-rooted properties, as a center or a

[2] These lines were written before 1939, before the articles which M. De. Corte has published since that time and which, in relation to some particularly important points, have developed a pseudo-theology in which we cannot acquiesce.

universe unto itself, a universe of productive vitality and spiritual emanation.

And so it is that if by a trick, by some kind of detour of the spirit, an experience of the self by the self succeeds in a supra- or para-conceptual way in grasping the subject and its intimate being, transferred to the state of an object, of a terminus of contemplative union, this experience will not constitute a poetic experience. But if an experience of the self by the self grasps the subject *as subject,* that is to say, in its quality of being radically and in living act the principle of productive vitality and spiritual emanation, then such an experience will be by that very fact a fecundation, as it were, of that very productivity. And such a grasp of the substance of the subject can only take place in a non-conceptual or non-logical mode, hence in an essentially obscure manner, at the very instant when some reality from the universe outside is grasped by mode of affective connaturality, in an intuitive emotion in which the universe and the subject are revealed together to the subject, as if by a beam of darkness. For it is in awakening to the world, it is in obscurely grasping some substantial secret in things, that the soul of man obscurely grasps itself.

That is the poetic experience or poetic knowledge, in which the subjectivity is not grasped as object by an explicit reflexion, but as source and *in actu exercito,* in the very process of grasping things by virtue of their resonance in the subject. It is a knowledge which is in its principle unconscious, a knowledge which is at the minimum of knowledge but at the maximum of germinative virtuality, a knowledge which is objectified completely only in the work, in an object made. It is an experience at the same time of the world and of the subjectivity, in which, to speak the scholastic jargon, the content most immediately grasped is the world, the content *most principally* (and most secretly) grasped is the subjectivity.

It is in this way, as we said above, that poetic knowledge is radically factive or operative, because, being inseparable from the productivity of the spirit (owing to the fact that the connaturality which awakens it actuates the subject as subject, or as center of productive vitality and spiritual emanation), it nevertheless cannot (because it attains the real only as buried in the subjectivity itself, and therefore non-conceptualisable) expand in a concept produced *ad intra,* in a mental word. Consequently, it can issue only in a work *ad extra.*

It appears then that the radical tendency of the poetic experience toward creation *ad extra,* in other words its belonging by origin in the line of art, must be related to its essential connection with the actual exercise of the subjectivity, rather than to the fact that the law of the poetic object is participation in existence and in existential pressure. Experiences other than the poetic experience are also experiences of existence (I am thinking of the Hindu contemplation of the Self), and even take place through a more purely existential approach and yet in themselves they are in no wise to be situated in the line of art and of the production of a work.

On the other hand, it follows from these considerations that poetic knowledge, though situated in the line of making, is all the same not *simultaneous with the poem itself.* Between poetic knowledge and the poem there is all the intellectual elaboration of art, whether voluntary or instinctive, whether primarily alert to listen or to act, and first of all there is that creative meditation which the original experience nourishes with its sap, and which is itself formed progressively and by degrees. The shock of poetic intuition can be received in the depths of the subject and remain there in a latent state; it can subsist thus for a long time. Or then, after that first moment of stirring the soul and falling into inertia, it can reappear later in the spiritual memory (which is *supra tempus*), without having lost anything of its power of emotion and of creativity. And finally, the poet can also, by going against the nature of things, turn this intuition aside from its operative ends, and seek by a kind of violence, and to his sorrow, as we have tried to show, to turn it into a pure knowledge. There is no poem without poetic experience. There can be poetic experience with no poem. (Although there is no poetic experience without the secret germ of a poem, however tiny it be.)[3]

II. *Existence and subjectivity.* M. Marcel De Corte has shown in a penetrating way that the poetic intuition is non-eidetic, alogical, existential. Must it be concluded from this that it has as its content naked existence, pure existence? All existence is the existence *of something*, for existence is in no way separable from nature or quality, from the intelligible stuff which exists; act and perfection of all acts and all per-

[3] It is because it demands of itself to take form in a poem, where it will be finished and manifested, as a fruit of the spirit, and revealed to itself, as an object of consciousness, that the poetic experience requires deployment in artistic activity. Already at the level of the artisan art turns toward deception, be it that of mass production or that of the fake masterpiece, if it is not born of some dynamic intuition which, though enclosed within the limits of a genre—weapon, jewel, tapistry, pottery, some work to be made—reveals to the heart the world of forms and merits in some way to be called poetic, as the connections made by the senses merit already being called *ratio*. In the case of the poet, to whose language (be it music, painting, the dance, architecture, or poetry) beauty, being transcendental, opens the infinite of being and of creation, art is a lie if during the whole extent of its act it does not remain the instrument of the poetic experience, and traversed by its life. Or rather—whether it seem completely instinctive and as if emerging from the unconscious, or whether it be characterized by all the knowledge and intelligence, the patience, the will, the ruse and the calculation that make of it a perfection of the working reason—it is nothing other, to tell the truth, than the poetic experience itself in the process of humanly bearing its fruit.

fections, the act of existing is itself, in truth, by reason of the potentialities for being which participate in it, something intrinsically varied, possessed of more or less intensity and generosity, and it is only analogically common to the diverse things that are. How could that which, under the creative influx, is the act par excellence of all things, in their most intimate and consistent as in their most fragile aspects, be denuded of things? If the eidetic intuition of the abstractive intelligence is incapable of grasping it apart from them, how could the poetic intuition do so?

In fact, the poetic intuition can do so less than any other, because it takes place by affective connaturality, by virtue of the resonance of that which is most existent and most concrete in things in that which is most existent and most concrete in the subject; and because it proceeds, not from some tense reflexive asceticism against the grain of nature, tending towards a kind of metaphysical death or release, but on the contrary from a natural and eminently spontaneous movement of the soul which is seeking itself in communing with things by means of the sense imbued with intelligence. Poetic withdrawal is as natural to the soul as the return of the bird to its nest, and it is the whole world which, with the spirit, comes back to the mysterious nest of the soul. Poetic intuition is radically productive, but productive of an object intrinsically and perfectly determined, and in some way necessary; and why is it thus, if not because it seizes, in order to express it in an object, not pure existence, but on the contrary some typical existent in its inmost self, buried in the creative subjectivity? The poetic emotion is sovereignly determined and individuated, and if poetry is, as Aristotle saw it, more philosophic than history, it is that it is akin to the most secret of the concrete, to the most intimate of essences, quiddities, qualities, talities, haececities, ipseities with which the real and the singular abound. And that is just why it, and the object made, abound in *signification,* deliver to the spirit at a stroke the whole universe in a single visage.

Il fallait bien qu'un visage
Réponde à tous les noms du monde.[3a]

It had to be that one face
Answered to all the names in the world.

In short, as M. Marcel De Corte himself tells us, "there is a really existing *quid* which experience seizes and mysteriously ravishes." But this *quid* is not seized by mode of quiddity, of essence, or of intelligibility; and that is what with good reason he wished above all to point out. Though the poetic experience is not of naked existence, its *mode* is all the same completely existential. As applied to the mode, to the manner of knowing, to the manner of seizing the real, no expression is too strong to separate the poetic intuition from the proper laws of the conceptual apprehension of essences. For, as we have seen above, the content of the poetic experience is grasped as *non-conceptualisable.* Thus it is the *mode* of this experience that is completely existential.

But even this is not enough—it is necessary to go further. The object also is existential, not in the sense that it is a naked existence to be grasped, but in the sense that the content of the poetic experience is not the terminus and final object of this experience; its final object is the work to be posited in existence, the work that is to be made to exist, it is a practical existential object.

Thus, one could say, the content of the intuition-emotion of the poet is like the *species impressa* of speculative knowledge: something essentially germinal and germinative. And it is the work made which is—terminus and final object—like the mental word or the *species expressa,* and like the reality known in the latter.

The poetic experience is not ordered toward seizing es-

[3a] Paul Eluard, *L'Amour la Poésie,* Paris, 1929.

sences, be it even in an existential mode, no! It is ordered toward expressing the subject, it awakens the subjectivity to itself in order that it may proffer itself, precisely by being transparent to some ray of being and in active communication with the world—however fleeting and slight, however small may be the ray which thus makes the contact. If it lets such a ray pass, an almost silent hai-kai is worth more than a great noisy machine for deciphering the alphabet of essences. The volume of the work counts, certainly, since in art it is itself a qualitative element. All things being equal in other respects, a large poem is worth more than a small one, but on condition of being just as humble and just as sensitive to the breeze as the divine little cloud of intuitive emotion in the subterranean sky of the poet. Poetry does not like noise.

There is a poetic knowledge of the world, but it is not for knowledge nor for knowing the world; it is for obscurely revealing to himself the creative subject, and fecundating him in his spiritual sources. If you pretend to use it for knowing, it vanishes in your hands.

> . . . Si je veux, je saurai vous dire
> Cela que chaque chose *veut dire*[4]

> . . . If I wish, I shall know how to tell you
> That which each thing *means*

Happily you do not wish it—that is more prudent of you.

> . . . Toute chose en moi devient
> Eternelle en la notion que j'en ai: c'est
> moi qui la consacre et qui la sacrifie.[5]

> Everything in me becomes
> Eternal in the notion that I have of it: it is
> I who consecrate and sacrifice it.

[4] Paul Claudel, *Les Muses.*
[5] Paul Claudel, *La Maison Fermée.*

To be exact, you do not have the *notion* of things, but the experience of them in you and of yourself in them. They do not become eternal in you, it is rather you who become visible in them. You are not here in order to sacrifice them but in order to suffer them, while they draw from you a sign of themselves and of you. The poet is not a hierarch who "calls all things to existence by giving to each thing its proper and everlasting name,"[6] that is to say by knowing it (prophetically) in its essence; he is rather a child who tames things by calling them affectionate names, and who makes a paradise with them. They tell him their names only in an enigma, he enters into their games, blindfolded, he plays with them at life and death.

Things are not just what they are; they pass unceasingly beyond themselves, and give more than they have, because they are traversed from every direction by the influx of Existence in pure act, and they love that Existence more than themselves. They are better, and worse, than themselves, because being superabounds, and because nothingness attracts that which comes from nothing. Thus they communicate in existence, under an infinity of modes and by an infinity of actions and contacts, of correspondences, of sympathies and malices, of breakings and reformings, and—insofar as they possess immateriality—of forms of interiorization of being and forms of giving. This communication in the act of existing and in the spiritual flux from which existence proceeds, a communication which is not certainly pure existence, and which is not the essences and the proper names either (though it presupposes them), but which is in things as if the secret of the creative sources, this is perhaps above all what the poet receives and suffers, in however small a measure

[6] Elsewhere M. De Corte remarks more justly: "It would be to misunderstand totally the nature of the act of poetic knowledge to identify it with a condensed act of intuition going further than rational knowledge, into the heart, into the intimacy of the object."

(but for a single stalk of that straw in the stable he would give all the rest), this is what he grasps without knowing it, or knows as unknown. *In finem nostrae cognitionis Deum tanquam ignotum cognoscimus,* say the doctors of mystical contemplation.[7] Of the poet one would have to say: in the principle of his creative movement he knows as unknown the communion of things (among themselves and with him) in the passages of spirit which make them be, and this is still another manner—quite different from the mystical one—of visiting with God.

Let us not say that the poet *fails* to know this mysterious communication, to know it as known, because in the order of nature he in no wise seeks to seize and hold it as known. Hidden in the spiritual unconscious, his experience is a knowledge which is not for knowing, but, from its very beginning and in its essence, for producing and creating.

In God himself we must—according to our mode of conceiving—distinguish between the knowledge "of simple intelligence" and the creative knowledge or the knowledge "of vision." In man this is a real distinction which, beginning at the very root, separates poetic knowledge from speculative knowledge.

III. *Poetic Knowledge and the sign.* In the poetic experience as in all existential and savory knowlege, in which the soul "suffers things more than it learns them" and which proceeds not *per modum cognitionis* but by mode of affective connaturality or of resonance in the subject, the emotion or inclination becomes a grasping of the real, *amor transit in conditionem objecti.* All the same this comes about in the case of poetic knowledge in a way unique and original to it and

[7] Cf. Pseudo-Dionysius, *Myst. Theol.,* cap. I, and the commentary of St. Thomas Aquinas.

quite otherwise than in the knowledge of mystical or infused contemplation, which is the highest example of knowledge by connaturality of love. In poetic knowledge the emotion or inclination issues in a grasping of the real, not in virtue of being a means employed by a *habitus* or an energy of the spirit (of faith, for example) which is already tending towards an object, towards a terminus in which to consummate objective union, but precisely in virtue of the fact that the emotion or inclination bears the real which moves the soul, the world which affects it and which it suffers, in the heart of its vitally productive subjectivity. And why is this? Because, we believe, in the case of the poet, unlike other men (especially those engaged in civilized life), the soul, considered not in its substance but in its powers and in their very root, remains, if I may express it thus, available to itself, keeps as it were a reserve of spirituality not absorbed by the world outside and by the *work* of the faculties; and this deep unused reserve of the spirit, being *unused,* is like a sleep of the soul; being *of the spirit* (which otherwise is occupied with things outside) it is itself in act, I say virtually, by way of a tension and a virtual reversion of the spirit on itself and on all that is in it. The soul sleeps but its heart is awake, let it sleep . . . And often it is in the ripeness of age, when the spirit has nourished itself with experience and suffering, and has made a return upon itself, that it knows this sleep best, a sleep which exists also, in another, more precarious, manner, with the too acrid greenness of youth, in the child and the primitive.

And so it is that when into the depths of such a secretly vigilant sleep and of such a spiritual tension, of such a dormant fire, emotion pierces—some emotion of the "vagabondage of individual existence," no matter what, it is *where it is received* that matters—the world it bears with it is received also, in the vitality of the waiting intellect virtually turned toward the substance of the soul and all its treasures.[8] It is then, at the very moment that it falls into the living waters, that the emotion becomes intentional and intuitive, and passes to the condition of a grasp of the real: not that it serves to objectify some term which specifies a knowledge, but because it is itself taken into the indeterminate vitality and productivity of the spirit, to which it brings a determination by mode of germ. The real and the subjectivity, the world and the whole of the soul coexist actively and inseparably in the emotion at that moment. At that moment sense and sensation are gathered back into the heart, the blood into the spirit, the passion into the intuition. And by the vital actuation of the intellect all the faculties are also actuated at their very root. It is the soul which is known in the experience of the world and it is the world that is known in the experience of the soul, by a knowledge which does not know itself, for where is the concept by which it could be objectified? What it knows, as we noted above, it knows as unknown, and not for the purpose of knowing but in order to produce. The objectification, if it takes place, will take place in the object made, in the work. It is toward a creation that this experience tends.

However imperfect the sketch here presented of an analysis of the poetic experience, we believe it will serve to point

[8] Thus it can happen that the poetic experience accumulates in the soul, which is quite unaware of it, like a great reserve whose pressure still remains without determinate effect. It will suffice then for some exterior occasion to present itself, a form thrown upon paper, a spot, a word, breaking the dam, for the whole mass to precipitate itself through the crack, and take form in falling. This apparently fortuitous inspiration is veritable inspiration because it emanates from the profound waters of a creative emotion accumulated little by little and whose potential may be very high; it has nothing to do with a simple psychological outpouring without a dynamic reserve of creative intuition, nothing to do with the pure unleashing of free association or of automatic writing, which strictly speaking, is its opposite. What is inspiration, if not the *spirit* of the poetic experience.

up several properties of that experience. As we have already noted, what is *most immediate* in it is the experience of the things of the world—because it is natural to the human soul to know things before knowing itself; but what is *most principal* is the experiencing of the subject—because it is in a knowledge of the self, however obscure, that that productive vitality is actuated in which emotion becomes intentional and sees. Let us add that it is not only from the love of charity, as in the case of the mystical or infused experience, but from any passion and emotion—even evil ones—and especially from grief, that the poetic experience proceeds. At the same time, the poetic experience would seem to maintain a more intellectual character than the experience of the saints, because the shock or the rapture which it makes the soul undergo, however vast and profound the concussion of it may be, tends at last towards an object which will be produced by the practical intellect, whereas the contemplation of the saints, proceeding from the transformation of love, tends toward love and toward a more perfect transformation.

Finally, the poetic experience departs from an object, an existent reality—that is why sense and sense perception are an indispensable condition for it—but not in order to make a return to the object like speculative knowledge, nor in order intellectually to become the object in a mental word and in judgments; no, it departs from the object in order to make a return to the spirit, and to the substance of the subject, and to go from there toward the object to be made. And if the content of the poetic experience is not its final object, it is not that that content remains exterior to the knowing subject, far from it—it is that it is *too* interior, that it is too inseparable from the subjectivity to be expressed other than in a thing which the soul will cast into being and into which it will cast itself and the world.

For if at the source of the poetic act there is the experience which I have tried to describe, in which the obscure grasping of the real, resounding in the creative subjectivity, is at the same time an obscure grasping of the soul of the poet, it will be necessary that the work made be a manifestation of both at once.

This work is an object, and must always maintain its consistency and its proper value as an object, and at the same time it is a sign, at once a "direct" sign of the secrets perceived in things, of their avowal, of some irrecusable verity of their nature or history, transpierced by the creative intuition, and a "reverse" sign of the substance of the poet in the act of spiritual communication and revealing itself to itself. And since all things communicate in being, and since being abounds in signs, in the same way this object will abound in significations, and will say more than it is, and will render present to knowledge, at the same time that it presents itself, something other than itself, and again something other than that other, and, at the furthest limit, the entire universe, as if in the mirror of a monad.[9] According to a kind of poetic amplification, Beatrice, while remaining the woman whom Dante loved, is also, by virtue of the sign, the Wisdom which conducts him; Sophie von Kühn, while remaining the dead fiancée of Novalis, is also, by virtue of the sign, the call of God which seduces him.

[9] That is the sense in which the Aristotelian notion of *imitation* must be understood, when from the most superficial and most empirical level one transfers it to the most metaphysical and most profound level. Because art is in itself a spiritual activity, this word imitation, which is a kind of trap, is related at the same time to that which is the most instinctive in art (the pleasure of imitating and of recreating forms, which is certainly more primitive in man than magic and the other super-added finalities), and to that which is the most subtle and spiritual in it (the *signification* of the object, insofar as it is the proper effect of the poetic knowledge of things).

Thus then there would be not a poetic work but a servile work if the object were only object. And if the object were only sign, there would not be a poetic work either, but allegory. And it is only through and in the object, through and in sensible signs in which the object abounds, that at the terminus of the poetic operation the content of the poetic experience is finally manifested and known in an express and communicable way. Having only a truth unproportioned to our intellectual grasp—since it is essential to it not to be conceptualisable, fleeting and impossible to seize by the means proper to the reason, it can only be brought into the light of consciousness, expressed and known in a communicable fashion, "through the symbolic mode," and by means of sensible figures which seduce the reason, according to the word of St. Thomas which we recalled above. In short, the object created by the poet is like the glory of the poet, and it is in this glory, through which he manifests himself to the world, that he manifests himself also to himself and becomes conscious in signified act, but in an inevitably imperfect and unsatisfying way, of his original experience.